Growing Among Us:

A Layman's Perspective

of the

Emerging Church Movement

Ronald A. Wright

Growing Among Us: A Layman's Perspective of the Emerging Church Movement

© 2009 Ronald A. Wright. All rights reserved. No portion of this book may be reproduced, stored in a retrieval system, or transmitted in any form or by any means – electronic, mechanical, photocopy, recording, or other – except for brief quotations in printed reviews, without the prior permission of the publisher.

Unless otherwise noted, Scripture quotations are taken from the Holy Bible: New International Version®. Copyright © 1973, 1978, 1984 International Bible Society. Used by permission of Zondervan. All rights reserved.

ISBN 978-0-578-01061-8

Published by:

BKK Publishing, LLC
136 Kempsville Road
Chesapeake, VA 23320

This book is dedicated to my wife, Wendi, and our children, Bryce, Kyle and Kalyn, without whose loving support I would never have been able to complete this or so many other projects.

Table of Contents

Introduction   3

Chapter 1 - Frogs and the Truth About 'Hard Water'   9

Chapter 2 - What is the Emerging Church?   19

Chapter 3 - A Brief History of Thought   31

Chapter 4 - The Rivers of Lake Emergent   43

Chapter 5 - The Second River: Praxis   57

Chapter 6 - The Third River: Postevangelical   75

Chapter 7 - The Fourth River: Political   93

Chapter 8 - A Proper Response   103

Introduction

In the fall of 2007, my Bible study group began to read a new book written by John MacArthur entitled "The Truth War". The book brought to light a new body of thinking that was rising within the church. It was known as the Emerging Church Movement, or ECM. It was an intriguing study for me, mainly because my good friend and former pastor had introduced me to many of the concepts through his sermons and other discussions. He was also a fan of Dr. D. A. Carson and referred often to his work when we spoke about the direction of the church in America today, and the up and coming generation of people whom the church would need to reach.

The more I read MacArthur's book, and the more I learned about the thinking within the ECM, the more I grew concerned. This concern was further reinforced as my current pastor discussed on various occasions the movement and its potential impact on our own church body. As I brought up the topic of the ECM when talking with other believers, I discovered that most had never even heard of it. However what I did find, to my alarm, was that those who had at least some exposure to the teachings within the movement simply accepted them as if they were perfectly correct. One friend eagerly shared with me about a video series that he said would transform my spiritual life. He often used the videos during a Bible study he led, and shared that all who attended truly enjoyed them. After doing a little digging I found that this was the "Nooma" video series put out by a man named Rob Bell. After viewing several of them I felt compelled to write a note of warning to my friend that he needed to look closely at what was being taught and what Bell himself actually believed.

I also brought up the ECM with my adult Bible study class at church. Our church is a conservative, Bible-based church with a traditional service style. So when I asked the question, "Who in here is familiar with the Emerging Church?" what I got back were a lot of questioning looks. Aside from a couple of friends who were in my Bible study group, nobody knew what the Emerging Church was; but they were definitely interested in learning more. Afterward, it was suggested that I do a short study for the class on the movement and how we should respond to it. I thought it would be a great opportunity for me to learn more on the subject as well, so I agreed to begin the study.

As I dug in to try and find information about the movement, I found that there was very little that had been formally written on it. In fact, the two main conservative sources that I found were MacArthur's book and another book by D.A. Carson entitled "Becoming Conversant with the Emerging Church". This second book was based on a series of lectures given by Dr. Carson at Cedarville University, my own alma mater, in 2003. However, rather than simply reading those who were considered critics of the movement, I really wanted to find out what those who were promoting it said that it was all about – and so that is where I began my research.

What I quickly came to see was that much of the information and discussions about the movement took place online in the form of blogs and on message boards. That, of course, is a dangerous place to find information since anyone can write anything and post it online to be read by the world. Eventually I was able to focus in on several of the more credible sources, and those led me to still others. What came to light was a movement that had many different facets, and it was difficult to truly understand any of it with just a cursory glance at what was being presented. To pin it down in any singular way was much like trying to nail jell-o to a wall. Even more disturbingly, as I delved deeper I found that some of what was happening was downright sinister in nature, as it focused on ways to lead the church in new directions simply through redefining terms and then claiming that we all believed the same thing (a sort of philosophical bait and switch tactic).

Perhaps the most frustrating problem that I ran into was that much of the terminology and discussions occurred on a level where most of us simply do not operate. I am a fairly well educated man, and have been involved in local church ministry for all of my adult life. While I am not an ordained minister I am a Bible college graduate and have served in many different roles within the local church. At the same time, I don't consider that I am any more involved or knowledgeable than most others at my church. My vocation is in the world of finance, not theology or philosophy. So while I would be comfortable discussing macroeconomics or investment analysis, the philosophical underpinnings of postmodernism in today's society just isn't part of my everyday conversations. I believed this would also be true of most others within the church. Unfortunately, much of the discussion and debate about the ECM is between academic scholars who jump quickly through arguments which they assume the reader would already understand. This makes it just that much harder to make sense of the movement.

This, then, is my reason for writing this book. My hope is that I will be able to explain what I have learned from my study of the ECM in a way that makes it easier for everyone to understand – not just those in PhD programs. I would also stress once again that what I am presenting here comes not just from a study of the criticism of the movement. As I mentioned earlier, I strove to find out what the leaders and proponents of the movement believe and are teaching. If I present things in a manner that seems unfair I would state very plainly that this is how it has been presented to me. If I misunderstand what is being taught, then I would encourage the leaders of this movement to redouble their efforts in helping us all to see a clearer picture of what they believe. However, I am confident that by and large I have presented an accurate picture of what is taking place. In addition, I would also heartily agree with Dr. Carson, who in the preface of his book on the movement makes this statement:

> "I have tried to be accurate in description and evenhanded in evaluation. Even so, I must underscore the fact that when I am forced (for the sake of avoiding endless qualifications) to resort to generalization in order to move the discussion along, one can almost always find some people in the movement for whom the generalization is not true, and others who do not think of themselves as belonging to the emerging church movement who nevertheless share most of its values and priorities."[1]

My goals for this book are simple: First, to provide at least a basic level of understanding of the movement and what those involved in it are teaching. Second, to provide a Bible-based analysis of those teachings. Third, to give some suggestions on how we in the Body of Christ can respond to this movement. And finally, but most important, to encourage us all to be ever more careful of what is being taught within our churches, schools, and homes. I would hope that we might all be like the Bereans in Acts 17. These early believers took it upon themselves to verify even what the Apostle Paul was teaching them:

> **_Acts 17:11_**
> [11]*Now the Bereans were of more noble character than the Thessalonians, for they received the message with great eagerness*

---
[1] D.A. Carson, *Becoming Conversant with the Emerging Church* (Grand Rapids: Zondervan, 2005) pg 12.

and examined the Scriptures every day to see if what Paul said was true"

Chapter 1

<u>2 Timothy 4:3, 4</u>

³For the time will come when men will not put up with sound doctrine. Instead, to suit their own desires, they will gather around them a great number of teachers to say what their itching ears want to hear. ⁴They will turn their ears away from the truth and turn aside to myths.

Frogs and the truth about 'Hard Water'

The Emerging Church is a topic that is neither easily nor quickly understood. Like others throughout church history, this new movement has many different facets. Some of them are positive, some are negative, and some are truly heretical. In order to illustrate the potential impact that the Emerging Church Movement (ECM) is having on the Body of Christ today, an example comes to mind. It is an old example that I'm sure we have all heard many times in the past: If you put a frog into a pot of hot water, it will hop right out. But if you put a frog into a pot of cold water and slowly heat it up, the frog will not notice the change until it is too late and he is already cooked.

But let's try it this way instead:

A frog named Steve lived out his life in the pond where he was born. There were other frogs around, but not all of them were like him. He believed, and rightly so, that he could get more sunlight and catch better flies if he lived his life on top of the lily pads rather than always swimming in the water beneath. Most importantly he had been taught that living only in the pond water would surely lead to death when the leaves fell and the cold air made the water turn hard. The food and sun were nice but it was the truth he had been taught about the hard water that made him stay on the lily pads.

Other frogs in the pond stayed in the water almost all of the time. After all, it took much less effort swim around and to catch the water bugs – even if they were a bit thin and somewhat unsatisfying. Moreover, they just didn't believe this whole 'myth' about the hard water. Some had heard the stories about it, but they believed them to be merely fairy tales. Steve tried to convince the 'swimmers' that all they had to do is hop up on the lily pads and they could enjoy the safety and the same great food as himself, but they were not easily convinced. Many times, in fact, they ridiculed him for his beliefs.

"Yours is not the only way to live," they would say. "This whole hard water thing is just a story, and your understanding is only one possible way to interpret it. We choose to listen to all of the ideas and form our own opinions."

One day, he met up with a new frog that had recently joined the pond. His name was Dave. Dave also believed that the flies were the best source of food, and he was very friendly. He was not so concerned about the idea of escaping the hard water however. For him, it was all about the good food and living a better life. He thought Steve had a good point in his interpretation of the hard water stories, but he did not entirely agree with it. Steve also understood that Dave didn't believe exactly the same as himself, but felt he could overlook it because in the end they wanted the same thing – for the 'swimmers' to be saved.

Steve and Dave eventually became good friends. Steve showed Dave all around the pond and showed him where all of the best lily pads were. He even introduced Dave to the other lily pad frogs he knew – telling them what a great guy Dave was. Eventually the two got around to talking about how to reach the 'swimmers' in order to convince them that they must come out of the water. Steve told Dave how hard he had tried to reach them, but they remained unconvinced that they might die if they remained in the water.

"Ah" said Dave, "The trouble is that you are using the wrong approach. These frogs need to be spoken to on a different level. You can't just scare them out of the water; you have to appeal to them in different terms – you have to speak their language."

And so Dave began to talk to the 'swimmers' about how great it was on the lily pads. He shared with them all that they were missing out on by staying in the water. He spoke about living a better, more fulfilled life on the lily pads. He was very careful not to insult them by saying his was the only way, but he insisted that it was the best choice for him – and he believed it would be the best choice for them as well. Slowly at first, some frogs decided to come out of the water and try the lily pads. Then over time even more joined them.

Steve was very impressed and wondered how Dave had made so much progress in such a short amount of time. He tried to talk to the new frogs, but they quickly backed away from him saying, "You're the mean guy who only wants to talk about how bad the water is and how the 'swimmers' have it all wrong. We really don't want to talk to you, you can just stay on your side of the lily pads and we'll be fine on our side."

This bothered Steve, because he saw that the other frogs weren't there because they accepted the truth, but only because Dave had told them they could enjoy an easier life. It was great to see that so many were joining him up on the lily pads, but he wondered if some really had any idea why they were there at all.

Steve believed in the stories about the hard water. He also knew from the stories that there would come a time when the flies would grow thin and the eating would not be nearly as good. That would also mark the time that it was most dangerous to go back into the water! He was afraid that if these frogs were only there for the food and the sun, then they would most certainly leave right at the worst possible time! He had to find Dave and get him to tell these frogs the truth.

After much searching, Steve was finally able to find Dave and talk to him about what was happening. He told Dave that the new frogs on the lily pads were not there because they knew the truth, but really because they just wanted to get the food. He also told Dave of his concern that the frogs would leave the pads when it was the worst possible time. These frogs needed to know the truth so that they would stay put even when times got rough.

"The truth?" Dave replied, "The truth is that the flies are the best food, and that these frogs have never had it so good. Sure, I know you have this thing about the hard water, but after all that is just how *you* choose to understand the old stories. The most important thing is that we let every frog taste the good life that we have here on the lily pads – right?"

"But Dave," said Steve, "If they don't realize that the hard water is the real danger, then they will leave the safety of the lily pads at the absolute worst time – right when the water gets ready to change. They will be trapped and die if they go back!"

"Oh, Steve" said Dave, "That is really such an old idea, and these frogs have so many other explanations for that whole 'hard water' thing. Most think it is really just a story meant to teach them to be more careful about where they make their homes. Others think it just means they need to be more adaptable. Really, Steve, you need to become a little more adaptable yourself. Just because you see the hard water one way does not mean that these others are wrong, they just see it differently. The truth is, it may be you that is wrong."

Steve walked away from the conversation saddened. How could he have allowed things to get so far out of hand? Even some of his old friends refused to speak to him now – they were drawn to Dave and the great success he was having in winning over the 'swimmers'. These old friends still believed the truth about the hard water, but they also believed it was better to stay quiet and not alienate themselves from the new frogs. They felt that by being more accepting of the new ideas, they could eventually win the new frogs over to the truth. But Steve saw that more and more of his old friends were joining in with the thinking of the new frogs and falling further away from the real truth.

The time finally came when Steve and the few who still believed in the old stories were no longer welcome to stay in their pond. Forced to leave their own homes because they were not open to the new ideas, they sadly hung their heads and sought out another pond in which to live. It was a sad time, but Steve and his friends knew they could not let go of the truth even though it meant leaving the others behind.

As you can guess, autumn eventually came, the air cooled, and the leaves began to fall. The food grew more and more scarce, but there was always just enough. The leaves that had fallen onto the lily pads provided shelter for the frogs against the cold winds that had begun to blow. Even still it was a tough time, and it seemed it would be so much easier just to hide in the pond water. At times the cold even seemed unbearable, but Steve and his friends remembered the truth and so they stayed on the lily pads.

Finally, the day came when the water turned hard. Steve and his fellow frogs were safe because they had chosen to stay on the lily pads. They often wondered how things had turned out at the other pond, and they planned a trip to see once the weather became warm again. The days went on, the frogs stayed in their shelters, and eventually the spring came and the water turned back to normal. Steve and several of his friends decided it was now time to check on the other pond.

As they made their way across the land they listened carefully for the sound of the other frogs croaking, but heard nothing. When they finally reached the water's edge their hearts sank as there was no movement in sight, only stillness and silence. They decided to do a quick search to see if they could discover what had happened. About halfway around the pond, they finally spotted some movement and quickly swam in to investigate. There, on a lone lily pad, was one of their old friends who had chosen to stay behind.

"What happened?" they asked, and he began to relate to them the whole sad tale.

"At first, everything was great. We all enjoyed life on the lily pads – even if it was a bit crowded at times. There was plenty of food and fellowship. But as the air began to cool, some of the frogs began to grumble. They said it was warmer and safer in the water, and the food was actually easier to find. Soon, many had returned to the pond. Then, when the leaves began to fall, others took it as a sign that we were not meant to stay on the lily pads, but that frogs were meant for the water. At the same time, the food was beginning to get scarce and even more frogs left the pads and returned to the water. Eventually, there were only a few of us left – just those of us who were on the pads from the beginning.

"One morning, we woke to find the most frightening sight of all. The pond water had become hard – just as the stories said it would. All of those frogs that had returned to the water were stuck. Most were caught under the hard water with no way to get out, and so they drowned. Some were caught halfway between so that they could see us, but they could not join us on the safety of the lily pads. Eventually, those died too. It was a terrible time for those of us that remained. We survived, but it was a horrible thing to watch.

"As time went on, most of us that remained decided to leave the pond and look for a new place to live. They simply could not bear the memory of all of those that died here. I am the last one left, and I was just about to leave to look for all of you myself."

Steve and his friends hung their heads in sadness. If only the other frogs had listened to the whole truth about the hard water. If only they had believed and not tried to explain it away as something else. They had only moved to the lily pads because of the promise of an easy life. As soon as the hard times came, they went right back to where they had come from, and that is where they died.

The problem surrounding the Emerging Church Movement is not that it is a threat to the survival of the traditional, mainstream church as some within the movement have suggested. It is not even that they bring to the forefront a call to revisit and perhaps change the traditional methods of the church in light of changing culture. The real problem is that much of the thinking in the movement, particularly the Emergent group, calls people to become part of just another religious system rather than calling them to faith in Christ alone as our means of salvation. They would say that it is more important to walk as Christ walked rather than spending so much time learning doctrine and studying the Scriptures.

The true danger lies in the possibility that we could fill our churches with lots of new people doing good things, yet none of them grounded in the truth and few who are truly members of the Body of Christ. These people are like the seeds that fell upon the rocks. They appear to have embraced the truth of the gospel, but when life becomes hard they have no root, nothing to sustain their apparent faith, and so they fall away. Jesus tells us that the path that leads to His kingdom, the path of truth, is the narrow one. The broad, easy path is the one that leads to ruin and destruction. Any movement that draws conclusions away from or stands contrary to the Word of God is most certainly pointing down the wrong path. That is not to say that truth cannot exist outside of the bounds of Scripture. But it is to say that any philosophy or ideology that contradicts or seeks to replace Scripture is categorically wrong.

Chapter 2

What is the Emerging Church?

So, you have heard about this new "Emerging Church" and would like to go and check it out. The first place most people look to find a church is in the phone book, so that is where you start. The funny thing is there is no "Emerging" section in the church listings. No problem, it must be that this church is so new it is not yet listed. So, you hop in the car and drive through town looking around to see which one of the churches has a sign that says it is an "Emerging Church", but again, no luck.

In fact, there is no Emerging Church denomination. Rather, it is a loose association of like minded ministries, each independent of any other outside authority. It is really better known as the Emerging Church Movement, or ECM, because it spans virtually all denominational boundaries. Many of the leaders within the movement prefer to call it a "conversation" because they like the openness and lack of formal structure that is implied. There are no pre-defined methods for worship or for the structure of church services. Rather, these ministries tend to reject traditional church services in favor of new and often very creative activities for worship. In some, members are free to roam around the facility and take part in various forms of worship which occur simultaneously. In one corner, the pastor may be leading a group discussion time. In another corner a praise band might be playing in a coffee-house style atmosphere.

There may be a prayer room set aside in another area and there may even be a movie or video series playing elsewhere. All of this would take place at the same time, allowing the attendees would move freely from place to place as they felt led.

Throughout all of this, it may be difficult to identify any specific organizational structure. The pastor/teacher will typically dress in a very casual manner as do the participants. Any ties to outside denominations would be carefully avoided. Even the names of the churches, such as Forefront Church or Symphonic or Apex, make it difficult to tell what they believe. Most also have very broad statements of belief or core values which again make it difficult to pin down where they stand on specific doctrinal issues.

As you can see, trying to pin down the ECM can be difficult. Part of that difficulty lies in the fact that they have developed much of their own vocabulary. To aid in the deciphering of the new terms that are used, I have included a short glossary at the end of this chapter. For those of us who grew up in the traditional church, and particularly in a conservative church, many of these terms as well as the philosophy that created them may be totally unfamiliar. In fact for most of us the basic ideology that is the focus of the ECM, postmodernism, is completely foreign to our own way of thinking. This makes it even more difficult for us to understand what the movement is and why those within it act the way they do.

A good starting point in learning just what the ECM is all about is to begin by looking at common elements that those involved within the movement share. It is important to remember that this is not a denomination, and as such there is no governing body that oversees the churches that are involved. Each one is free to practice however they see fit, but they do tend to have these overall themes in common.

Common Themes of the Emerging Church

1. *A rejection of the mainstream, traditional church.*

The basis behind the formation of the ECM would seem to be a response to the general state of the church in America today. Many of the leaders involved in the formation of the movement saw a general decline in churches in America, and an even greater problem when trying to reach the younger generation and bring them into the church. The secularization of our society has left the youngest generation without any clear concept or understanding of faith in God and what the church is supposed to be. The initial goal of the founders of the movement was to find a way for the church to once again become relevant in the thinking and lives of the younger generation.

Part of the focus then became trying to reach out and meet this new generation where they live (outside the trappings of a traditional church setting). Another part turned to look within the church itself to see how it could and indeed must change in order to reach this new culture. This is why ECM churches tend not to have any strong denominational ties, even though they may have come directly out of a church that is part of one. Their focus is squarely on the group they are trying to reach, not on maintaining church or denominational distinctives. ECM churches also tend to have less formal lines of authority, choosing instead to have more of a community feel where everyone can have a say in what is taught. Because of this, many emerging churches actually begin within the walls of existing mainstream churches and eventually break off to form their own identity.

2. The belief that changes in culture drive changes within the church

In response to the changes that take place over time within any given culture, the ECM believes that a new church should, even must, emerge from the old in order to meet the needs of the new generation – thus the name Emerging Church. Dr. D.A. Carson, in his book on the ECM, addresses this theme very clearly:

> *At the heart of the "movement" – or as some of its leaders prefer to call it, the "conversation" – lies the conviction that changes in culture signal that a new church is "emerging." Christian leaders must therefore adapt to this emerging church. Those who fail to do so are blind to the cultural accretions that hide the gospel behind forms of thought and*

> modes of expression that no longer communicate with the new generation, the emerging generation.[1]

3. A genuine desire to reach postmodern culture.

The postmodern philosophy is a new body of thinking that is quickly taking hold and defining the next direction for our society and culture. The roots of the ECM come from a sincere desire to reach postmodern thinkers with the gospel and to bring them back to the church. That is certainly a good and necessary goal if the church is to fulfill its role in the great commission. The problem is that postmodern thinking is so foreign to traditional church culture that there is no easy way to reconcile the two. The result is that the ECM has been viewed as a sort of underground movement within the traditional church, and therefore in many ways is misunderstood. This disconnect has caused unnecessary divisions in some areas, and the blind acceptance of bad or even heretical teachings in other areas.

4. The belief that how one acts is more important than what one thinks (or even believes).

One of the main problems that the ECM identified in the traditional church was that there was a lot of talk about addressing problems, but not a lot of action. Of course, this has been an accusation against the church

---

[1] D.A. Carson, *Becoming Conversant with the Emerging Church* (Grand Rapids: Zondervan, 2005) pg 12.

since the beginning – that the church is filled with hypocrites that act one way on Sunday and totally different Monday through Saturday. Within the ECM, the focus has shifted to "living the way of Jesus" rather than studying and learning what the whole of Scripture teaches. The focus then becomes that of imitating what Christ did rather than seeking to understand why He did it.

5. ***The idea that social justice should be a major focal point of church ministry.***

Because of their great focus on the actions of Christ, the idea of social justice becomes a major focal point for the ECM. Social justice has many connotations, but generally speaking it means caring for those who are less fortunate and working to restore the world to its proper order, as God had originally created it. The idea here is that if the church was acting as God intended, then we would see His kingdom in practice on the earth right now. Poverty, hunger, homelessness, and even racism would all become things of the past. This concept is also strongly related to the political views of many within the movement, particularly the more liberal Emergent thinkers.

6. ***The concept that truth is seen through the perspective of the individual, so that how one person perceives truth may be completely different from another – yet each can be correct.***

The ECM recognizes the fact that we all carry with us our own intellectual baggage. That is, my understanding of Scripture may not line up with yours simply because of our varied backgrounds and the different churches we did or did not grow up within. Moreover, they feel that our understanding of the original biblical languages is most certainly weak at best, so there is no way we can be absolutely certain we have the one true interpretation of Scripture. Therefore, the best possible option in understanding spiritual truth lies not in a deeper study of the text, but rather in seeking out and trying to understand all of the possible interpretations. If we gather all of the interpretations together, then we may begin to catch a glimpse of the real truth by trying to synthesize all of the pieces into one. This can be seen in the emphasis on community rather than a formal leadership structure within ECM churches.

In addition to these common underlying themes, there are several forms that ECM churches can take. As is the case even within most denominations there are those churches which are more conservative and of course there are those that are more liberal in their theology. D.A. Carson tends to separate the forms into three camps: Confessional, Heterodox, and Middle Ground[2]. The Confessional group consists of those who are Bible-based and evangelical in their approach, and still grounded in good theology. These are seeking to bring the gospel to groups that lie outside the mainstream church in both lifestyle and thinking, with the goal of bringing them to faith in Christ. The second group, what he calls the

---

[2] Taken from Vanguard Church Blog "DA Carson versus the Emerging Church" by Bob Robinson (vanguardchurch.blogspot.com/2007/03/)

Heterodox group, is the other extreme. These represent the part of the ECM that is truly devoted to the ideals of postmodern thinking and have built their theology around it (the implications of this will become much clearer later on). The third group, Middle Ground, is a balance of the first two.

Another way of looking at the forms that emerging churches take comes from Mark Driscoll[3], pastor of Mars Hill Church in Seattle, Washington and one of the early participants in the movement. He believes that churches within the movement can be grouped into four different categories. The first would be the emerging churches, which are those who are part of the ECM but would still fall within Carson's confessional or middle ground camps. The focus of this group is simply to reach postmodern thinkers and others outside of the mainstream church with the truth of the Gospel. The second category is the house church form, which throws off traditional settings in an attempt to reach those outside the mainstream church. These are still basically evangelical in their approach but they reject traditional church settings and formalized structures. The third group consists of traditional churches which have adopted a more contemporary worship style or added a contemporary service to their traditional Sunday morning service. The final group is the Emergent or Emergent Village, which are the truly liberal thinkers within the ECM. These would fall firmly within Carson's Heterodox group. This group openly questions and even denies conservative doctrines such as the atonement,

---

[3] Interview with Mark Driscoll,
http://www.desiringgod.org/media/video/2006_National/national2006_driscoll_interview1.mov

the authority of Scripture, the exclusivity of Christ, and in some cases even the deity of Christ.

Let me be clear at this point that there are many within the Emerging Church Movement that are doing good. Pastors such as Mark Driscoll and others involved in the Acts 29 community have been specifically highlighted, even by the critics of the ECM, as striving to do good work. They are in the group that stays true to the study of God's Word and have separated themselves both willingly and publicly from the teachings of those in the Emergent Village, which is the truly liberal side of the movement. Within the Emergent group, men such as Brian MacLaren, Doug Pagitt, Rob Bell, Chris Seay, and others are presenting teachings and ideologies that are truly dangerous. These are the teachings that we must stand firmly against as they try to make inroads into our churches and our homes.

Favorite Terms of the Emerging Church Movement:

- **Conversation** – the movement is really a "conversation" that discusses and compares different ideas about what to believe and how to go about "doing church". For the Emergent, it includes the belief that "...All theology is always a conversation about the Truth who is God in Christ through the Spirit. It is never final, it is never fixed."[4]
- **Story** – revelation is given in the form of a story rather than hard fact or teaching. We all have a story in ourselves, and we all need to learn from other stories as we journey through our own.
- **Nuance** – truth cannot be known with certainty, and so any hard edged teaching must be softened or nuanced in order to make it fit with other possible truths.
- **Emergence or emerging** – a new version of the church comes to light with each new cultural shift, but it needs to grow and adjust to the new culture in which it rises or "emerges".
- **Postmodernism** – a philosophical system that rejects the idea that objective truth can be known with certainty, among other ideals.

---

[4] Scot McKnight, *What is the Emerging Church?* (Fall Contemporary Issues Conference, Westminster Theological Seminary) October 2006, pg 24.

- **Community** – the group of people that interact together in order to share ideas and develop a "correct" interpretation of truth.
- **Missional** – the community is focused on participating with God in the redemptive work God is doing in the world. The focus is on transforming the world around them in order to restore it to God's ideal and to correct social injustices that are now present.
- **Mystery or Mystic** – the Emergent rejects traditional dogma and doctrine and instead embraces the mystery of God and His revelation. In this, the Emergent rejects the idea that any truth can be known with absolute certainty or that any belief system is self-sufficient.
- **Orthopraxy** – the Emergent believes that how a person lives is more important than what they believe. They seek to "practice the way of Jesus" rather than define standards or doctrines based on a systematic theology.
- **Justice** – defined as "the condition and behavior that conforms to the will of God"[5] (as interpreted by the emergent believer). Social Justice is a major theme of the ECM and is closely tied to the Missional idea, the goal of which is to reconcile the world to God through correction of injustices that exist everywhere.

---
[5] McKnight, pg 18

Chapter 3

John 18:37-38
³⁷"You are a king, then!" said Pilate.

Jesus answered, "You are right in saying I am a king. In fact, for this reason I was born, and for this I came into the world, to testify to the truth. Everyone on the side of truth listens to me."

³⁸"What is truth?" Pilate asked. With this he went out again to the Jews and said, "I find no basis for a charge against him.

A Brief History of Thought

When the ECM first began to take shape, those involved in its formation shared a common goal. That was to reach the new generation of Americans that the mainstream churches were missing. There was mounting evidence to suggest that the church had lost touch with the generation-x crowd, and those coming up behind them were now virtually untouched by both the church and the gospel. The main cause that they were able to identify for this problem was that there had been a drastic change in the way this new generation thought about and experienced life around them. This new philosophy is called postmodernism, and it represents the first major shift in our thinking since the rise of Modernism in the late 19th century.

In order to understand just what postmodern thinking means, it is very helpful to go through a quick study of how we got to where we are today. John MacArthur, in his book "The Truth War" provides an excellent synopsis of the history of thought over the past centuries from the perspective of the church, and D.A. Carson provides an even more detailed explanation in his own book on the emerging church. My goal in this chapter is simply to provide a summary of the different philosophical periods in order to get a basic idea of where postmodernism comes from.

Starting points – the Ancient Greeks:

The study of how we learn about and understand the world around us really begins with the rise of great thinkers and teachers such as Socrates, Plato, and Aristotle. These men formed the basis of a body of philosophy known as naturalism. Those who held to naturalism believed that all knowledge is conveyed through nature or through natural means. In other words, man gains knowledge by observing what is going on around him. This, of course, is the easiest and most basic way that we learn. This basic philosophical viewpoint is still around in various forms today, and provides the foundation upon which the other, newer philosophies are built.

Next steps – the Enlightenment

The next major shift in our understanding of thought and knowledge came during the enlightenment. Building upon and refining the ideas developed in naturalism, philosophers such as John Locke brought forward the idea that all knowledge is derived from experience. This includes both inner experience such as thinking and reflection of the mind, and outer experience or perception of the world around us through the senses. This new philosophy was called empiricism. An important aspect of empiricism is the belief that the mind starts out as a blank slate, with no innate or pre-conceived ideas, and knowledge is acquired completely through the five senses and then stored within the mind.

Another competing philosophy also rose to popularity at this time, which became known as rationalism. Rene Descartes and other rationalists believed that we all have some innate or inborn understanding of foundational truths, and that by using logical deductions and reason mankind builds upon this understanding. The contrast between the rationalists and empiricists lies in the focus of where knowledge comes from, either from basic self evident truths or from our perception of the world around us.

Immanuel Kant looked at both of these philosophies and saw that each had validity in different areas. He believed that man is born with an innate sense of right and wrong (rationalism), but also learns from his surroundings, circumstances, and experiences (empiricism). Kant worked to synthesize the two viewpoints in his own critical philosophy. Within that, he presented the idea that man understands the existence of a moral law, which is external to himself. However, man also acts based upon what he sees and experiences around him. Those experiences many times lead man to find ways to act in opposition to the external moral law in order to gratify his own desires.

Where most of us are – the Modern Era

The next shift in thinking came about during the late 19th and early 20th centuries. This was known as the rise of modernism. Modernism built upon the ideas offered up during the enlightenment, but shaped them through the advent of the industrial and scientific revolutions. The positive side of the modern era was the quest for objective truth and knowledge. Academics began to focus on separating myth from fact and tradition from logic and reason. They sought to discern the why behind how things worked, to understand the forces behind the world in which we live. This led to many scientific discoveries that have transformed the way we live today, most particularly in the area of healthcare. Just imagine what it would be like if we still believed in bloodlettings for the treatment of various illnesses. It is difficult to imagine today what could have possibly led physicians to believe that could be a cure for anything.

But all of that advancement also had a negative side. With their focus on logic and discovery, mankind began to reject the Bible as a basis for truth, replacing it instead with the scientific method. First, a hypothesis about a particular observation is created, and then an attempt is made to either prove or disprove that hypothesis. For example, the observation is made that chicken soup helps to aid the recovery from the common cold. A scientist then forms a hypothesis as to why this might be so, and systematically goes about testing to see if that hypothesis can be proven or disproven. A true student of the scientific method is just as happy to have a hypothesis disproven as proven because either course leads to greater knowledge and understanding.

This form of thinking eventually developed into the philosophy known as rationalistic presuppositions, which is virtually synonymous with modernism. The concept of a presupposition is that every thought or understanding must have a starting point. For those of us who hold to the Bible as the starting point of knowledge, one of our presuppositions might be that God created everything. However, modern thinkers would consider that to be an irrational presupposition because one can neither prove nor disprove the existence of God. Therefore, they begin with the presupposition of the big bang, and point to surrounding evidence that appears to support their belief. In truth both are unprovable ideas which require a measure of faith. We cannot scientifically prove the creation account any more than the evolutionist can prove the big bang. Neither one can be re-created within the laboratory or anywhere else for that matter. But the modernist points to a preponderance of evidence to suggest (rather firmly) that their presupposition is more rational than that of the creationist. In other words, they would argue that while the evidence for their position is still circumstantial, there exists so much of it that it must be true even though it cannot be proven through recreating the same event.

An unfortunate result of this thinking was a renewed interest in criticism of the Bible. Scholars began to apply scientific methodology to the scriptural accounts of creation, the flood, and other major events in an attempt to disprove the authority of the scriptures. A rational view of the

Bible began to gain ground which called into question the validity of things such as miracles as well as the accuracy and legitimacy of many of the historical narratives (such as creation, the virgin birth, the resurrection, etc.). After all, miracles by their very nature defy logical explanation; otherwise they would not be miraculous. Academic scholars and rationalists felt that if something could not be explained through logical means, then it must simply be a myth or some other kind of fictional account. This new view of the Bible led from the belief that God is the ultimate revealer of all knowledge to the belief that it is up to mankind to seek and discover everything for himself. So for the modernist who holds to rationalistic presuppositions, it is human reason that determines truth. Following this to its logical conclusion leads down a path through doubt, the rejection of faith, agnosticism, and finally into humanism and atheism, where man himself becomes the center of everything.

The next generation – the Postmodern Era

Near the end of the 20th century, a new philosophy began to take shape to explain how man perceives and experiences the world around him. The fathers of postmodernism looked at the ideals of modernism and saw that there were indeed problems and inconsistencies. Modernism promised that mankind would be forever moving forward toward a utopian ideal where knowledge ruled supreme and gave us everlasting peace. It was supposed to end all wars, cure all social inequities and set us on the path toward ultimate enlightenment, something like the world of 'Star Trek' where all mankind worked together for the common good. Modernism also tried to force the realm of the supernatural (i.e.: religion) out of existence, seeking to replace it with logic and reason.

But in the end, Modernism made promises upon which it simply could not deliver. It also dismissed truths about faith and other non-scientific belief systems on the basis that they did not fit into a rational philosophy. Philosophers began to see that science apart from faith leads to a dead end. There were questions about life and truth that existed outside of logic and reason which pure science simply could not answer. The main battleground for the postmodern thinker therefore became that of seeking out the truth, regardless of where it may be found. The question to be answered is: Does there exist an objective, absolute truth about life and is man capable of knowing it?

The postmodern thinker contends that while an absolute truth may exist, man, because of his lack of complete objectivity, cannot be certain as to what that truth is. We all have preconceptions and shortcomings through which we filter our experiences of the world around us. Those preconceptions lead us each to specific conclusions, but they may not be the only possible conclusions. Others, who have a different set of preconceptions, may view the same experience in a completely different light, yet it is the exact same experience. For example, imagine with me that I had in my possession a note card which was blue on one side and red on the other. Now, suppose I held the card up for two people to see, but did it in such a way that each could only see one side of the card. When I ask the two people to describe the card, one would very confidently say that it is red, and the other would say that it is unmistakably blue. Each would be correct insofar as their own experience and observation could take them, but neither would be completely correct in their assessment. Postmodern thinkers believe that this is the very same problem that we each have in trying to grasp absolute truth.

The postmodernist believes that it is impossible for a person to be entirely objective in their thinking simply because each of us has come through different life experiences and educations that cloud our judgment in one way or another. A person who was raised within the church will have their thinking clouded by what they have been taught just as much as one who was raised in a purely secular environment. What this means is that by ourselves we are unable to come to an unbiased complete understanding of what is true. What we need is the knowledge and experiences of others in order to fill in the gaps within our own understanding.

Taking this to its logical conclusion, this means that there can be no exclusive claims on the truth, such as the belief that faith in Jesus Christ alone is the only means of salvation. The postmodern thinker would suggest that you may have a sincere faith in Christ, and that your belief may be partially correct, but the beliefs of a Buddhist or a Hindu would also have aspects of spiritual truth within them which cannot be ignored. Therefore, no one person can say they have an exclusive claim to the truth. As a result, all views must be given equal validity.

In all of this we cannot ignore the influence of the internet and other tools that have brought us to a new level of interconnectedness in modern life. The younger generations have grown up using email, chat rooms, and instant messaging to such an extent that they begin to feel uncomfortable when forced to face an issue in isolation. This need for interconnectedness further reinforces the postmodern emphasis on community and a 'group think' paradigm versus individual discovery.

At this point, we can divide the postmodern philosophy into two basic camps. The first are the hard postmoderns. These believe that the subjectivity of the human mind makes it completely impossible to know and understand absolute truth. Hard postmodernism is quickly identified by a myriad of disclaimers like, "as I see it" or "as I understand or perceive it" or "as far as we are able to know". Often this is referred to as having a proper confidence or a chastened epistemology (to use philosophical terms). The other camp is that of the soft postmoderns. These would agree that it is impossible to have an absolute grasp of truth. However, they also believe that it is possible to get close enough to that truth to say we have captured it with a high degree of certainty. In other words, we may not be 100% correct, but we might get to 98%, which is close enough to say that there is no substantial difference.

The postmodern thinker, whether hard or soft, also has a true dislike for the idea of a propositional statement. A proposition is an either/or argument, which implies there is a right and a wrong answer. For example, a woman can either be pregnant, or not pregnant. There is no such thing as being just a little bit pregnant. The concept of propositional truth is deeply ingrained within modernism with its focus on the scientific method. A hypothesis is either proven or disproven. If the outcome is questionable, then further testing is required in order to come to a firm conclusion. Propositions are also quite comfortable for those of us in the church because we see right and wrong clearly outlined in Scripture. But postmodernism views all human understanding as subjective and flawed, so by its very nature it rejects the idea of propositional truth. Note that it does not embrace the idea of relative truth, meaning that right and wrong can change within the context of the situation. Rather, postmodernism states that we cannot completely know any singular truth because we cannot be wholly objective.

Because of this clouded perception of the truth, the postmodern tends to embrace the idea of mystery or mysticism. They would suggest that some things just cannot be explained, they simply need to be believed. It might be easy to see this as a return from hard secularism to faith in spiritual things, and it has certainly opened up the door for what the modernist would call irrational presuppositions. However, that does not mean that there will be a sudden move toward accepting by faith the gospel of Christ and the teachings of the Scriptures. Rather, for the postmodern thinker it means that we simply cannot know all there is to know. That being the case, we must be willing to accept the mystery of some things without concrete explanation, realizing there is no way we can come to a complete understanding of them. Consider the rise over the past decade in the acceptance of psychics and other supernatural phenomenon. There are even prime-time television shows today that are based upon or are entirely devoted to those topics.

While the modernist strives to prove or disprove everything, the postmodern says, "Let's just accept that it exists, embrace the mystery of it, and move on." John MacArthur sums up this thinking when he writes:

> *"The goal of human philosophy used to be truth without God. Today's philosophies are open to the notion of God without truth – or to be more accurate, personal 'spirituality' in which everyone is free to create his or her own god. Personal gods pose no threat to sinful self-will, because they suit each sinner's personal preferences anyway, and they make no demands on anyone else."*[1]

The verses at the beginning of this chapter show that this thinking is not really new at all, just newly re-packaged in a more intricate way. Pilate himself asked Jesus the question, "What is truth?" At the core of postmodern thinking is the rejection of the idea that we can know objective truth, and know it with certainty. However, that is most definitely not what the Bible teaches us. In fact Scripture constantly challenges us to seek the truth and promises that we can know it.

Luke 11:9-10
[9]"So I say to you, ask, and it will be given to you; seek, and you will find; knock, and it will be opened to you. [10]"For everyone who asks,

---

[1] John MacArthur, *The Truth War* (Nashville: Nelson, 2007), pg 8

receives; and he who seeks, finds; and to him who knocks, it will be opened.

John 14:6

⁶*Jesus answered, "I am the way and the truth and the life. No one comes to the Father except through me."*

John 17:17

¹⁷*Sanctify them by the truth; your word is truth.*

Chapter 4

2 Peter 1:20-2:3

[20]Above all, you must understand that no prophecy of Scripture came about by the prophet's own interpretation. [21]For prophecy never had its origin in the will of man, but men spoke from God as they were carried along by the Holy Spirit.

[1]But there were also false prophets among the people, just as there will be false teachers among you. They will secretly introduce destructive heresies, even denying the sovereign Lord who bought them—bringing swift destruction on themselves. [2]Many will follow their shameful ways and will bring the way of truth into disrepute. [3]In their greed these teachers will exploit you with stories they have made up. Their condemnation has long been hanging over them, and their destruction has not been sleeping.

The Rivers of Lake Emergent

As I began my study of the ECM, I found that most of the information surrounding it was in the form of blogs and message boards on the internet. My goal through this study was to find information presented by those within the movement that described what it was from their perspective, so that is primarily where I looked to find what I was seeking. The most obvious reason behind the principal use of the internet by the ECM is because it allows ideas to be introduced much more quickly and easily than through traditional print materials. It also allows for open and ongoing discussion of the ideas among many different participants. The downside is the difficulty in determining which sources are credible and which are not.

After some searching, I was able to uncover a concise academic summary of the movement in the work of Dr. Scot McKnight. Dr. McKnight is a professor of religious studies at North Park University in Chicago. He is a major advocate and speaker for the ECM and runs a web site known as *Jesus Creed*. Within that web site, I was able to find a copy of an address that he gave at the Fall Contemporary Issues Conference at Westminster Theological Seminary in October of 2006. The address was entitled: "What is the Emerging Church?"[1] In fact, within it McKnight himself brings forward the idea that the best way to understand the movement is to listen to what is being said by those who are part of it, so it was just what I was looking for.

In order to describe the movement, McKnight draws upon the image of a lake, which he calls "Lake Emerging". Flowing into this lake there are four distinct rivers which highlight different aspects of the emerging church:

River #1 - Postmodernism

River #2 - Praxis (the way we go about "doing" church)

---

[1] Scot McKnight, *What is the Emerging Church?* (Fall Contemporary Issues Conference, Westminster Theological Seminary) October 2006.

River #3 - Postevangelical (protesting evangelicalism)
River #4 - Political

His lake metaphor highlights the diversity that is present within the movement. Each of these rivers attracts different people and, as McKnight illustrates, some choose to stay on their preferred river or at least near the mouth of that river, while other people go straight on into Lake Emerging and embrace the whole mix. This provides an excellent picture of the complexity of trying to describe the movement with just one or two phrases.

The First River: Postmodernism

We looked at the roots of postmodern thinking in the previous chapter, so we don't need to re-visit that here. Looking at the postmodern river in terms of the ECM, we instead want to see how that philosophy impacts the thinking of those within the movement. If you will recall, a basic premise behind postmodernism is that, because of our own limitations, we cannot know objective truth with certainty. Within the ECM, this means that the integrity and authority of Scripture is one of the very first casualties. Instead, the focus when looking at Scripture (or any other religious text for that matter) is to understand it as a narrative or a story. In the same way, we should view our own lives as a story that is just now being lived out. The goal of the reader is to interpret the stories of scripture in light of their own personal story and find common ground with others and their own personal stories. McKnight comments on it in this way:

> "...postmodernity as a philosophy forces upon the postmodern person the admission that our 'stories' are embedded in space and time, and the confession that our community and our faith determines where our minds journey."[2]

In other words, there is no set starting point or ending point. All of our stories are embedded in space and time, meaning they exist at a specific time and place. But they should be considered part of a complex tapestry of stories woven together so that for the whole of them there is no beginning or end. This thinking also suggests that there is no single foundational truth upon which to build our belief systems, at least not one that is demonstrably better than any other. This in turn creates the need for a community focus in order to join many stories together so as to create a sort of consensus. Because of this, or maybe in order to better facilitate this, the ECM puts an emphasis on embracing the mystery of spirituality as opposed to the study of doctrine and theology. It is most certainly easier to believe that there are things which we simply cannot explain than to devote oneself to the study of the underlying theological truths. Also, the study of doctrine gives rise to propositional truth, which we already know to be abhorrent to the postmodern philosophy that guides the ECM.

Interestingly, this is an area where those in the ECM believe that they and the evangelical church should be on common ground. After all, accepting things without having to prove them certainly sounds a lot like the idea of faith:

---

[2] Ibid, pg 11

Hebrews 11:1

[1]Now faith is being sure of what we hope for and certain of what we do not see.

We in the evangelical church accept by faith the integrity and authority of the Bible, and we believe that salvation comes through faith alone in Christ Jesus. Those in the ECM would contend that this is the same principal at work within their idea of embracing the mystery of things. The key difference is that we believe in the exclusive authority of Scripture as the foundation for our faith, while they view the Bible as just one more narrative among many. This is an important distinction. The postmodern thinker looks at many different spiritual narratives (the Bible, the Koran, even the book of Mormon) and applies to them the belief that understanding must come by means of the interpretation of the reader rather than discerning the intent of the writer. This may at first seem like a contradiction, but it does fit with the postmodern philosophy. Remember, postmoderns maintain that because of our own shortcomings, we cannot objectively know what the intent of the author was. Therefore we are left to interpret each narrative story in light of our own personal stories as well as the stories of those around us. Our own interpretation will undoubtedly be insufficient by itself. We will need to balance our own thinking with that of as many others as possible in order to arrive at the best possible conclusion. The obvious problem with this is that it leaves fallen man to determine which of God's truths are to be obeyed and which were really just suggestions about how we might live our lives.

This is not to suggest that those involved in the ECM merely turn off their brains and float through life ignorant and happy. It is quite the opposite in fact. If gaining clearer knowledge of any spiritual truth requires understanding all of the ideas surrounding it, then one must be devoted to in-depth studies of all of the thoughts and stories about that subject. The end result is endless learning and questions with no final answer to any of them. This entails not so much the idea of trying to be inclusive of all other ideas, but rather the rejection of any idea that claims to be exclusive. For example, you and I might have very different ideas about which type of drink is better – Coke or Pepsi. So long as neither claims to be the only real cola drink, then we can work together in the postmodern world. We may not like the other drink, and even choose not to drink it out of personal preference. But as long as we don't outright reject it, we can co-exist. However, if someone comes along who claims that RC Cola is the one and only real cola drink, and that the others are merely imposters, then that person would not be accepted into our group because they are trying to make an exclusive claim. In the thinking of many within the ECM, to claim that your belief system is the only right way is nothing short of pure arrogance.

Within the river of postmodernism, McKnight identifies three different categories of ministry. The first are those who seek to minister *to* postmoderns. These are Christians who are seeking to reach postmodern thinkers in order to teach them the truth of the gospel and see them come to faith in Christ. They view postmodernity as a philosophy out of which people must be rescued. More importantly, they often see postmodernism as a philosophy that is at odds with the clear teaching of the Scriptures. A good example of this kind of ministry would be a traditional church that also has a contemporary praise and worship service alongside their traditional services. The intent of such a ministry would be to open a dialog with the postmodern thinker while still maintaining strong ties to their own belief system and the truths of scripture.

    The second category is made up of those who minister *with* postmoderns. The motivation driving these ministries is not simply to rescue people out of postmodernity, but instead to walk along side them and guide them toward understanding the truth of the gospel. McKnight refers to this as a "*paracletic* as opposed to *parasitic* form of ministry"[3]. This group believes that postmodernism is an inescapable fact of life, and as such we are the ones who need to adapt in order to reach the world around us. They would suggest that the church needs to adjust its practices in order to relate to the new generation. Note that they are not necessarily arguing for outright change in the basic doctrines of the church. Rather they would try to soften certain doctrines in order to make them more palatable for the postmodern mind. Those in this second category might point to the example of Paul when he says:

> <u>*1 Corinthians 9:20-22:*</u>
> *[20]To the Jews I became like a Jew, to win the Jews. To those under the law I became like one under the law (though I myself am not under the law),*

---

[3] Ibid, pg 12

> so as to win those under the law. ²¹To those not having the law I became like one not having the law (though I am not free from God's law but am under Christ's law), so as to win those not having the law. ²²To the weak I became weak, to win the weak. I have become all things to all men so that by all possible means I might save some.

McKnight is careful to point out that the vast majority of emerging churches fall within these first two categories, but there is a third group as well. The final category consists of those who minister *as* postmoderns. McKnight describes this group as "the sexy kind"[4]. These have chosen to fully embrace the ideals of postmodernism and all that it entails. This third category is by far the most liberal part of the movement, and it is where you will find those who are part of the group known as Emergent Village, or simply Emergent. The Emergent Village embraces ideas that run from merely liberal to truly heretical. Central to the thinking of this kind of ministry is the idea that we must question each and every doctrine and rethink all of the facets of the Christian faith. They believe that the whole of the Christian faith, not just its methodologies, must evolve with the culture around it in order to remain relevant.

A great example of this line of thinking is the book "Velvet Elvis" by Rob Bell. In illustrating his point about maintaining the relevancy of Christianity within a changing culture, Bell uses the example of a painting of Elvis that he has tucked away in his basement. His premise is that the church, if it does not change with the times, will become just like that

---
[4] Ibid, pg 13

painting. What at one time seemed like the epicenter of cool is now just an eyesore that gets hidden away from sight. In his introduction, Bell writes:

> "For thousands of years the followers of Jesus, like artists, have understood that we have to keep going, exploring what it means to live in harmony with God and each other. The Christian faith tradition is filled with change and growth and transformation. Jesus took part in this process by calling people to rethink faith and the Bible and hope and love and everything else, and by inviting them into the endless process of working out how to live as God created us to live."[5]

Be certain that you don't miss Bell's characterization of Christianity as "The Christian faith tradition". This is just the first easy step down a very slippery slope. By fully embracing the ideals of postmodernism, those who minister as postmoderns must by necessity reject the exclusivity and authority of the Bible. Bell himself does this in a couple of ways. First, he states very clearly that he believes the Bible is open-ended. He writes:

> "So if we are serious about following God, then we have to interpret the Bible. It is not possible to simply do what the Bible says. We must first make decisions about what it means at this time, in this place, for these people."[6]

And further:

> "The Bible tells a story. A story that isn't over. A story that is still being told. A story that we have a part to play in."[7]

---
[5] Rob Bell, *Velvet Elvis: Repainting the Christian Faith* (Grand Rapids, Zondervan) pg 11
[6] Ibid, pg 46
[7] Ibid, pg 66

To be fair, Bell does not seem to be saying that there is more of the Bible to be written such as some others might suggest. Rather, he is falling back on the postmodern viewpoint that the interpretation of the reader overrules the intent of the author. It is this method of interpretation that allows the Bible to be open-ended because each reader can find their own meaning within the context of their own lives.

Second, he diminishes the authority that the Bible has over us as Christians:

> "The Bible is a collection of stories that teach us about what it looks like when God is at work through actual people. The Bible has the authority it does only because it contains stories about people interacting with the God who has all authority."[8]

When you put these thoughts together, what comes out is the concept that the Bible is a book of stories that gives us guidance, which we are to interpret according to our own surroundings and circumstances, and then put to use to help us live out our own lives. It does not have authority over us to reprove or compel us toward certain actions or beliefs. It does not have authority because it is God's inspired Word given to man. Instead, the idea is that through it God is sharing things about how He interacted with people in the past, so that we can learn from them and hopefully make our own interaction with Him better today. This certainly stands in contrast to the idea Paul presented in his second letter to Timothy:

---

[8] Ibid, pg 65

> *2 Timothy 3:14-18:*
>
> [14]*But as for you, continue in what you have learned and have become convinced of, because you know those from whom you learned it,* [15]*and how from infancy you have known the holy Scriptures, which are able to make you wise for salvation through faith in Christ Jesus.* [16]*All Scripture is God-breathed and is useful for teaching, rebuking, correcting and training in righteousness,* [17]*so that the man of God may be thoroughly equipped for every good work.*

In the book of Hebrews, the writer actually admonishes the readers for their lack of study and understanding of the Scriptures and encourages them to move on toward maturity in that knowledge:

> *Hebrews 5:11-6:1a:*
>
> [11]*We have much to say about this, but it is hard to explain because you are slow to learn.* [12]*In fact, though by this time you ought to be teachers, you need someone to teach you the elementary truths of God's word all over again. You need milk, not solid food!* [13]*Anyone who lives on milk, being still an infant, is not acquainted with the teaching about righteousness.* [14]*But solid food is for the mature, who by constant use have trained themselves to distinguish good from evil.*
>
> [1(a)]*Therefore let us leave the elementary teachings about Christ and go on to maturity*

Within the conservative church, there is a doctrine that speaks to the issue of the clarity and understanding of the Bible. It is known as the doctrine of the perspicuity of Scripture. Don't let the name scare you off, it is actually much easier to understand than to pronounce. Dr. Larry Pettigrew of The Master's Seminary put together a very good summary of the doctrine in an article he wrote for The Master's Seminary Journal in 2004[9]. In it, he breaks the doctrine down into eight different aspects. I'll summarize them here, and would suggest a reading of Dr. Pettigrew's article for a more detailed explanation.

According to Pettigrew's article, the doctrine of the perspicuity or clarity of Scripture means the following: First, it means that as a whole, Scripture is clear enough for even the simplest person to live by. It is possible for everyone to understand the basic truths that are being taught. Second, it means that Scripture is also deep enough to challenge readers of the highest intellectual ability. Third, Scripture is clear in essential matters. This would include things such as the concepts of sin, repentance, salvation, etc. Fourth, it means that any obscurity that one might find in some parts of the Bible are entirely the fault of the reader and of sinful mankind. Fifth, perspicuity means that any interpretation of Scripture must be done by ordinary means (as opposed to supernatural or extra biblical revelation). Sixth, it means that even an unsaved person can understand the Scriptures on an external level. Seventh, it means that the Holy Spirit must illumine the mind of the reader in order for the Bible to be completely and correctly understood. And eighth, the doctrine of perspicuity means that every Christian has both the privilege and the responsibility to read and seek to understand the Bible for themselves. This is so that their faith rests upon the authority of Scripture and not that of the church or any other institution or tradition.

---

[9] Larry D. Pettigrew, *"The Perspicuity of Scripture,"* The Masters Seminary Journal 15/2 (Fall 2004), pg 209-225

Finally, let me conclude our look at the first river of Lake Emerging, postmodernism, with this thought. The idea that we need to view God's Word with skepticism and interpret it according to our own personal point of view is not new – not by any means. In fact, it goes right back to where the whole problem started:

Genesis 3:1-6

¹ Now the serpent was more crafty than any of the wild animals the LORD God had made. He said to the woman, "<u>Did God really say</u>, 'You must not eat from any tree in the garden'?"

² The woman said to the serpent, "We may eat fruit from the trees in the garden, ³ but God did say, 'You must not eat fruit from the tree that is in the middle of the garden, and you must not touch it, or you will die.' "

⁴ "You will not surely die," the serpent said to the woman. ⁵ "For God knows that when you eat of it your eyes will be opened, and you will be like God, knowing good and evil."

⁶ When the woman saw that the fruit of the tree was good for food and pleasing to the eye, and also desirable for gaining wisdom, she took some and ate it. She also gave some to her husband, who was with her, and he ate it.

Chapter 5

> *James 2:14-18:*
>
> [14]*What good is it, my brothers, if a man claims to have faith but has no deeds? Can such faith save him?* [15]*Suppose a brother or sister is without clothes and daily food.* [16]*If one of you says to him, "Go, I wish you well; keep warm and well fed," but does nothing about his physical needs, what good is it?* [17]*In the same way, faith by itself, if it is not accompanied by action, is dead.*
>
> [18]*But someone will say, "You have faith; I have deeds." Show me your faith without deeds, and I will show you my faith by what I do.*

The Second River: Praxis

According to Scot McKnight, the second river flowing into Lake Emerging is that of Praxis. Praxis is a philosophical term which refers to the way we do things, so what McKnight is speaking about is the way we go about "doing" church. He believes this river is where we really get to the heart of the ECM, which is 'living the way of Jesus'[1]. Recall that in the mind of a postmodern thinker, what one does is more important than what one believes. Within the ECM there is a greater emphasis on what we are doing in our churches than on what we are teaching. This is undoubtedly in

---

[1] Scot McKnight, *What is the Emerging Church?* (Fall Contemporary Issues Conference, Westminster Theological Seminary) October 2006, pg 14

response to the belief that the church is full of hypocrites who act one way on Sunday and in a completely different manner Monday through Saturday. One must admit this argument has some validity. Hypocrisy has always been part of the church because it is part of man's sinful nature. The answer to that dilemma for the emergent believer appears to be to fully acknowledge that the disparity exists, and then work toward doing better – in other words, to 'keep it real'.

The ECM is highly critical of the church for the way we present ourselves to the world. Those outside the church see us building bigger and bigger buildings while always asking for money. They see libraries full of theological books and seminaries producing great biblical scholars. And they also see poverty and hunger in our streets, yet the church appears indifferent to it. They see great racial divides on Sunday mornings. They see arguments over abortion rights and politics, but the single mother often gets forgotten in the process. Much of this seeming disparity is just a matter of perception, but to the individual perception is reality. So at the individual level, the argument for placing practice over doctrine begins to make a lot of sense.

McKnight breaks the concept of Praxis down into four individual focus points: Worship, Orthopraxy, Justice, and Missional. These build upon one another and blend together to form the entire notion of Praxis – prescribing how the emergent believer will go about performing the ministry of the church. It is important to point out that not every idea that the ECM brings to light is bad. Many emerging church congregations are doing great work in their communities. We just need to be aware of the thought processes behind those ideas in order to determine whether or not they fall in line with biblical teaching. If they do, then we in the mainstream church should consider how to put them into practice in our own lives. If they do not, then they must be re-evaluated or even outright rejected.

The first focus point of praxis, worship, is by far the most public and well known. Worship in ECM churches can be very different than in the traditional church. Many times, worship for the ECM takes a trip back in time to revive imagery, creeds, and symbolism that most evangelical churches have long abandoned. For example, the memorization and recitation of the great creeds of the faith are completely absent from the worship services of most conservative evangelical churches. Some even shape their services very carefully so as to avoid emotional responses. In contrast, emerging church worship tends to place a far greater emphasis on emotional imagery and symbolism. In many cases that imagery also includes a twist on things to show that they are still rejecting old-line traditionalism. For example, during the Christmas season an old bike tire was used in place of an advent wreath at the base of a candle during one emerging church worship service.

ECM worship times are often multi-sensory in nature. They may include the simultaneous use of group discussion, music, candles, incense, prayer rooms, and even forms of physical activity. The goal in this type of setting is to enable the individual to break free from the bounds of tradition and to involve the whole person in the act of worship.

The sermon or teaching time during these services also takes on a different approach. Recall from the overview of the first river that with postmodernism there is a great deal of emphasis on community and shared experiences. The goal is to bring together all of the thoughts surrounding a spiritual concept, so that the group as a whole can get closer to the actual truth within that concept.

Doug Pagitt, pastor of Solomon's Porch in Minneapolis, has written a book about this approach to teaching, entitled *Preaching Re-Imagined*[2]. In that book, he presents the model of progressional dialogue during the church service as a replacement for the traditional sermon. Pagitt believes that the sermon, delivered from the pastor to the congregation, is one of the worst possible ways to gain spiritual understanding. He argues that preaching, which he calls 'speaching' is nothing more than one man engaging in one-way communication to a group of people. In place of speaching, he argues for progressional dialogue, which he describes thus:

> *"Progressional dialogue...involves the intentional interplay of multiple viewpoints that leads to unexpected and unforeseen ideas. The message will change depending on who is present and who says what. This kind of preaching is dynamic in the sense that the outcome is determined on the spot by the participants."*[3]

---

[2] Doug Pagitt, *Preaching Re-Imagined: The Role of the Sermon in Communities of Faith* (Grand Rapids, Zondervan, 2005)
[3] Ibid, pg 52

He also writes:

> "In many ways, the sermon is less a lecture or motivational speech than it is an act of poetry – of putting words around people's experiences to allow them to find a deeper connection to their lives. As we read through sections of the Bible and see how God has interacted with people in other times and places, we better sense God interacting with us. So our sermons are not lessons that precisely define belief so much as they are stories that welcome our hopes and ideas and participation."[4]

I hope that you can begin to see how the beliefs brought forth within the first river, postmodernism, are driving the actions in the second river, praxis. Remember that those who embrace postmodernism also reject the explicit authority of Scripture. Once that authority is repealed, then all points of view have equal validity and therefore must be examined in order to properly interpret the Bible according to each individual's own story.

Progressional dialogue encourages just that. Instead of a pastor delivering an expository sermon to the congregation of his church, there is a time for the mutual sharing and interpretation of a passage of Scripture. Picture if you will a group of friends talking about a spiritual topic over a cup of coffee outside of the local Starbucks. The meanings derived from that passage are determined not by what is written or even by the context of the passage, but rather by those who are present and by the individual

---

[4] Ibid, pg 166

viewpoints that they represent. Once again we see the interpretation of the reader superseding the intent of the author.

Imagine for a moment that you took a group of five year olds, put them in a room, and had them give their own interpretation of this passage:

Acts 28:1-6

[1]*Once safely on shore, we found out that the island was called Malta.* [2]*The islanders showed us unusual kindness. They built a fire and welcomed us all because it was raining and cold.* [3]*Paul gathered a pile of brushwood and, as he put it on the fire, a viper, driven out by the heat, fastened itself on his hand.* [4]*When the islanders saw the snake hanging from his hand, they said to each other, "This man must be a murderer; for though he escaped from the sea, Justice has not allowed him to live."* [5]*But Paul shook the snake off into the fire and suffered no ill effects.* [6]*The people expected him to swell up or suddenly fall dead, but after waiting a long time and seeing nothing unusual happen to him, they changed their minds and said he was a god.*

Without any frame of reference, those children might come to the opinion that the islanders were entirely correct in their understanding of the events. But just because a group reaches a consensus does not mean that they have uncovered the truth of the matter. They might even have concluded that the whole bible was a book about a god whose name was Paul who came to Earth to do battle with snakes! At first blush that may seem like an extreme example, but then again maybe it isn't. The group of people that the ECM is trying to reach may have no more knowledge of

Scripture than any group of five year olds. In fact, depending on the individuals forming the group, they may have even less!

Progressional dialogue is not about the speaker imparting knowledge to the hearers. The goal is to bring together as many ideas as possible about a given subject, and through this to achieve a unity of understanding for the group. In essence it is a pure democracy of thought. It is important to note that each group could come to its own unique understanding, completely different from every other. No one would blame the kids in the example above for coming to the wrong conclusions. They were simply trying to understand the story based upon their own limited knowledge and experience.

This is the very problem with progressional dialogue. It assumes that the participants already possess sufficient understanding of the topic in order to come to a valid interpretation. But if those participants are there in order to learn new things, it is more than likely they don't have such an understanding. The answer to that problem is quite simple: Put someone into the room who is able to teach them what the story is really about, what the author is actually trying to communicate, and thereby lead them to the proper conclusions.

One of my family's favorite television shows puts different urban legends to the test to see whether or not they are true. One of the episodes tested different myths about how to fool police radar in order to avoid speeding tickets. They tested several ideas including shooting tin foil confetti from an air cannon, blasting microwaves back at the radar beam, and repainting the car flat black in order to absorb the radar signal. In the end not one of these ideas worked – the radar gun clocked the correct speed of the vehicle each and every time.

In the world of progressional dialogue, the thought of putting those myths to the test would likely not even be considered. Actually testing ideas brings about a propositional (true / false) argument, which is contrary to the whole dialogue concept. Coming to a conclusion actually brings the dialogue to a close, and leaves us with a right and a wrong answer. The emergent thinker would find that to be extremely arrogant, believing it is impossible for any of us to know enough to make that kind of determination. Instead, they would prefer to gather people together to talk about the various ideas and decide through that forum which might or might not work.

In the end the group may come to a decision that for them, the flat black paint is the best way to fool the radar. But the truth is that no matter how much or how sincerely they believe it will work, they will still be just as wrong. This is the problem with using progressional dialogue as the center point of learning within the worship context. It can and often does lead to belief systems that are far removed from the reality of Scripture.

The second focus in the area of praxis is what McKnight refers to as Orthopraxy. Orthopraxy is just another way of saying "the right way to live". McKnight is very forthright when he addresses this issue as he states:

> "To be straight up about it, the emerging movement thinks how a person lives is more important than what they believe, that orthopraxy is the most important thing. And that the power of a life forms the best apologetic for the way of Jesus."[5]

In saying this, McKnight is correct in one sense. Our actions should bear witness both to whom we follow and to our faith. The book of James is very clear on this point when it states:

> **James 2:14-18:**
> [14]What good is it, my brothers, if a man claims to have faith but has no deeds? Can such faith save him? [15]Suppose a brother or sister is without clothes and daily food. [16]If one of you says to him, "Go, I wish you well; keep warm and well fed," but does nothing about his physical needs, what good is it? [17]In the same way, faith by itself, if it is not accompanied by action, is dead.
> [18]But someone will say, "You have faith; I have deeds." Show me your faith without deeds, and I will show you my faith by what I do.

To be fair, McKnight is not arguing that the ECM believes in salvation through works. Instead, he is arguing that the church needs to be actively engaged in doing good things rather than sitting in a classroom learning doctrines and tired old traditions. Those in the ECM believe that there is simply no way for us to get our theology 100% correct. They point out that even great scholars will argue about various points and see the same Bible passages in different ways. Because of this difficulty, the emergent believer simply declares the theological questions to be a

---
[5] McKnight, pg 16

mystery, and instead turns the focus on practical application rather than on knowledge or belief.

This line of thinking is closely related to another area of philosophy known as existentialism. For example, an existentialist might say, "I am who I am because of what I do." The response of a Christian, who submits to the authority of God and His Word, would be, "I do what I do because of who I am." If we have been redeemed by God, and are now slaves to His righteousness, then our lives should demonstrate that fact in everything we do. However, the emergent believer rejects the absolute truth and authority of the Bible. This is based on the premise that we cannot know objective truth because of our own limitations. Therefore if the external authority of Scripture is removed, we are left with nothing to define ourselves other than how we act. If we act in kindly ways, then we are good. If we act in evil ways, then we are bad. So if we seek to act the same way that Jesus did while He was on the Earth, then we must be Christians – right?

Rob Bell uses the analogy of jumping on a trampoline in order to illustrate this point. He compares the Christian life to a trampoline and Christians to those who are jumping on it. In his view, the most important aspect of the trampoline is not that we understand what makes it work or holds it together. We don't need to know the spring tensions or the methods behind manufacturing the fabric or the specific composition of the metals in the frame. He believes the most important thing is that we get on and start to jump. He calls this "living the way of Jesus", which is a very common phrase within the ECM. Here is how he describes it:

> "As a Christian, I am simply trying to orient myself around living a particular kind of way, the kind of way that Jesus taught is possible. And I think that the way of Jesus is the best possible way to live...Jesus at one point claimed to be "the way, the truth, and the life". Jesus was not making claims about one religion being better than all other religions. That completely misses the point, the depth, and the truth. Rather, he was telling those who were following him that his way is the way to the depth of reality. This kind of life Jesus was living, perfectly and completely in connection and cooperation with God, is the best possible way for a person to live. It is how things are."[6]

Scot McKnight states that orthopraxy is not an argument for salvation through works, but what he and others are proposing is every bit as damaging. By stating plainly that how a person lives is more important than what they believe, he removes any foundation for the action. Put another way, if belief does not direct action, then the action in and of itself is empty of meaning. It is exactly the opposite of faith without works, it is works without faith. Jesus speaks clearly about the end result of such actions:

> **Matthew 7:22-23**
> [22]Many will say to me on that day, 'Lord, Lord, did we not prophesy in your name, and in your name drive out demons and perform many miracles?' [23]Then I will tell them plainly, 'I never knew you. Away from me, you evildoers!'

---
[6] Rob Bell, *Velvet Elvis: Repainting the Christian Faith* (Grand Rapids, Zondervan) pg. 20,21

We are not called to good works simply for the sake of creating a better world. Our world is already full of secular organizations with that very purpose. Should the church try to emulate them? We are called to do good works so that through them we will bring glory to our Lord and Savior, and then draw others to become worshippers of Him along with us. Our works are to be driven by what we believe, not the other way around.

By focusing so intently on living the way of Jesus in order to become closer to God, emergent thinkers fall into the same trap that the Pharisee's own love of the law led them into so many centuries ago. The law was not given to mankind in order to become the central focus of our faith, but instead to demonstrate the need for something external to the law. By showing us our inability to overcome sin through perfect obedience, the law points us to the need for a better way – that of salvation which is provided through faith in Jesus Christ alone. In the same way, trying to live as Jesus did in order to become closer to God misses the point: Jesus _is_ God. He wants us first and foremost to know Him, and then He will take care of the business of transforming our lives to become like His own. It simply doesn't work the other way around.

The practical application of the concept of orthopraxy in the ECM begins to manifest itself through the third focus point in the river of Praxis: Social justice. The idea behind social justice is that it is the responsibility of the church to promote justice in our world on behalf of God. McKnight defines justice in this context as "…the condition and behavior that conforms to the will of God"[7] The specific area of the will of God with which the ECM appears to be most concerned is that of caring for the poor and looking out for the interests of those who are weak or otherwise unable to look out for themselves.

Social justice concerns itself with fixing what is wrong with society and our world. The idea is that the church is to be God's means of restoring the world to where it should be, to where it was before the fall. In working toward social justice, the ECM seeks to alleviate poverty and put an end to racism and cultural prejudice. There is also a strong impetus toward ending war and other types of conflict. Finally, there is also a growing emphasis on environmental awareness and stewardship of the Earth. Certainly these are all noble goals and no one could seriously argue against them. The problem is that, just as in the concept of orthopraxy, all of these things can so easily just become empty works. It doesn't take a Bible believing Christian to do these things – even the most ardent humanist can do good works and promote world peace. But it is also true that Christians should be involved in these types of things, as an outward demonstration of their faith.

In pursuing social justice, the ECM seeks to be multicultural and highly inclusive in all areas of practice. This goes beyond having more than one ethnic group represented in their congregations. It means welcoming belief systems that differ from their own and accepting all kinds of alternative lifestyles. After all, ending all conflict and prejudice means that

---

[7] McKnight, pg. 18

every belief or point of view must be heard and given proper respect. To reject someone on the basis of their personal belief system or lifestyle would be exclusionary, and contrary to the nature of postmodern thinking. In his book, *A Generous Orthodoxy*, Brian McLaren makes the following statement which seems to relate directly to this idea:

> "Although I don't hope all Buddhists will become (cultural) Christians, I do hope all who feel so called will become Buddhist followers of Jesus; I believe they should be given that opportunity and invitation. I don't hope all Jews or Hindus will become members of the Christian religion. But I do hope all who feel so called will become Jewish or Hindu followers of Jesus."[8]

The obvious problem with this goal is that it sets Christianity equal to any other religious practice in the world. The gospel of Christ makes an exclusive claim: *"For there is no other name under heaven given to men by which we must be saved (Acts 4:12)."* However, the emphasis in postmodernism says that exclusivity is both arrogant and presumptuous, and throws open wide the gate for any other belief system to join in. This creates a kind of syncretistic faith system which tries to combine elements of all into one. The final determination of just what to include is left up to the preferences of the individual.

This brings us to the final focus point in the river of Praxis: being missional. Though they would prefer not to be called evangelistic, emerging churches most certainly do go about sharing their faith and beliefs. This is

---

[8] Brian McLaren, A Generous Orthodoxy (Grand Rapids: Zondervon, 2004) pg. 264

part of what it means to be missional, but the concept includes far more than simply going out and witnessing to the lost. McKnight describes it thus:

> "The central element of this missional praxis is that the emerging movement is not attractional in its model of the church but is instead missional: that is, it does not invite people to church but instead wanders into the world as the church. It asks its community, 'How can we help you' instead of knocking on doors to increase membership."[9]

One of the greatest arguments given against evangelical Christianity is that the entire goal is to get someone to walk the isle, pray a prayer, get baptized, and join the membership roll. After that, they are on their own. The charge is that evangelicals are only worried about getting people saved, not about helping them in their daily life. In many cases the effectiveness of a ministry is measured by the number of people who are baptized each year, and the names of church members are only removed from the rolls when specifically requested. It doesn't matter if they have not been part of that church in years (or sometimes if they aren't even still alive). The whole focus of the ministry becomes that of 'soul winning', so that in the end discipleship (and in many cases compassion) gets lost along the way. When that happens, it is no wonder the world sees nothing but a bunch of Bible thumpers.

For the ECM, being missional entails far more than just evangelism, though that is definitely one aspect of it. Emerging churches see God doing

---

[9] McKnight, pg. 21

His redemptive work in the world, and they seek to join with Him in that work. Redemptive work also means far more to them than just bringing salvation to the lost. It includes everything that must be done in order to restore the world to what it was before the fall. The ECM sees this as the holistic redemptive work of God.

Emerging believers point to the work that Jesus did while He was on the Earth as the ultimate example of how to put their faith into practice. Jesus went about caring for the sick, the poor, and the outcast. He healed both the broken body and the broken spirit. At the same time He rejected those who oppressed others in the name of religion and fought for the rights of those who could not fight for themselves. So when Jesus said that He came "To seek and to save that which was lost", He meant far more than just making it possible for people to go to heaven when they die. The ECM believes that we are called to this broader work of reconciliation and redemption as well.

Another aspect of being missional involves the surrounding community, and provides for the practical application of social justice. Emerging churches seek to perform their role in the redemptive work for their community through their local body of believers. Their hope is that the church would have such an impact on their community that if it were suddenly to be removed, those around them would feel the loss deeply. To them church is not just a group that gets together twice on Sundays and occasionally on Wednesdays. It is where people live every day and interact with each other and with God; and most certainly not to the exclusion of those around them who aren't even members of that particular church body. It is to be a community of believers existing within and providing benefits to the broader community where it ministers.

So the second river flowing into Lake Emerging, called Praxis, is oriented around how the emerging church goes about doing its work. It involves the areas of worship, daily living (orthopraxy), social justice, and outreach (missional). This second river builds upon the postmodern philosophy which flows through the first river and provides practical outworking based upon that thinking. The focus becomes that of doing good things while relegating understanding and beliefs, which give real spiritual value to those good works, to a distant second place. One cannot argue that doing good works is inherently wrong, but the Bible teaches us plainly that good works alone are simply not enough.

Chapter 6

> *2 Timothy 4:3-4*
>
> ³*For the time will come when men will not put up with sound doctrine. Instead, to suit their own desires, they will gather around them a great number of teachers to say what their itching ears want to hear.* ⁴*They will turn their ears away from the truth and turn aside to myths.*

The Third River: Postevangelical

The third river feeding into Scot McKnight's Lake Emerging is called Postevangelical. Of the four rivers that he describes, this one is by far the most troubling. In its efforts to re-define Christianity in order to reach the new postmodern culture, the ECM has become oriented around a protest rather than striving toward a goal. What the ECM is protesting is, quite simply, the traditional mainstream church, with special emphasis on the evangelical church. McKnight puts it like this:

> "...the emerging movement is a protest against evangelicalism, and to make the lines clear the emerging movement often defines evangelicalism in simple, un-nuanced terms... So, let me begin with a simplification: the gospel is more than Jesus coming to die for my sins so I

can get to heaven. This gospel is not only protested by the emerging movement, it is rejected."[1]

As the movement adopts the posture of a protest, the thinking and the writing become more critical and anti-oriented. This meshes very well with the basic thrust of postmodernism, which is: question everything. Eventually this line of thinking pushes the arguments in some very disturbing directions. The point of asking questions changes from trying to gain a better understanding of spiritual truth, to that of discrediting older thoughts and ways of doing things in order to replace them with new, more exciting ones. This is evident in the statement above, where McKnight declares that the ECM is rejecting that which the Bible states is the very core of the gospel as we understand it. He sees the movement as reacting to the evangelical church with a "been there, done that" mentality. This seems to imply that they are basically just interested in wrecking the old ways and simply starting again from scratch with newer and more exciting ideas. They don't seem to be concerned at all that the old ways may well be correct, and the new ones wrong.

One might also question the use of the prefix 'post' that is being used here. The idea behind the prefix is that the emerging movement is actually the next evolution of the Christian faith. For example, in the same way that a telephone is 'post' the telegraph or a car is 'post' the horse and buggy, the ECM is 'post' evangelical. So when an emergent thinker states

---

[1] Scot McKnight, *What is the Emerging Church?* (Fall Contemporary Issues Conference, Westminster Theological Seminary) October 2006, pg. 22

that they are postevangelical, they believe that they have moved beyond evangelical Christianity to the next higher plane of spiritual thinking.

Emergent writers in particular tend to go to extremes in order to encourage us to throw off the shackles of the old way of thinking and free our minds to new possibilities. As an example, here is an excerpt from Rob Bell's book "Velvet Elvis":

> "What if tomorrow someone digs up definitive proof that Jesus had a real, earthly, biological father named Larry, and archeologists find Larry's tomb and do DNA samples and prove beyond a shadow of a doubt that the virgin birth was just a bit of mythologizing the Gospel writers threw in to appeal to the followers of the Mithra and Dionysian religious cults that where hugely popular at the time of Jesus, whose gods had virgin births? But what if as you study the origin of the word virgin, you discover that the word virgin in the gospel of Matthew actually comes from the book of Isaiah, and then you find out that in the Hebrew language at that time, the word virgin could mean several things. And what if you discover that being "born of a virgin" also referred to a child whose mother became pregnant the first time she had intercourse? …Is the way of Jesus still the best possible way to live?"[2]

Bell creates arguments from fanciful ideas that are specifically designed to make the readers question their beliefs. This is a little like asking a politician, "How long has it been since you stopped beating your spouse?" It doesn't matter if that person had never done any such thing; the intent of the question is to undermine their credibility and to plant doubt in the hearer's minds. The goal for the ECM isn't really to test the old

---

[2] Rob Bell, *Velvet Elvis: Repainting the Christian Faith* (Grand Rapids, Zondervan) pg 26-27

ideas to see if they are true or if they hold up under scrutiny. Rather, the goal is to clear out the old in order to make way for new, seemingly better ideas.

The result of this style of questioning, and intentionally so, is to chip away at the foundational doctrines of our faith. And at the same time that emergent thinking discourages in-depth bible study, it encourages action over knowledge and belief. The net result is a manner of thinking which places form over substance and in turn leads to poor views of the basic doctrines of the Christian faith. In the above example, Bell calls into question the doctrine of the virgin birth by creating fictitious arguments that exist directly in opposition to the testimony of the Bible itself. If we remove the foundations of our faith, brought to us by God's Word, then we are lost indeed.

Of course, the accusation that the miracles of Christ were just stories made up by the apostles is not a new one. In fact, the apostle Peter answered Bell's questions more than 2000 years ago when he wrote:

> **2 Peter 1:16-21:**
> [16]We did not follow cleverly invented stories when we told you about the power and coming of our Lord Jesus Christ, but we were eyewitnesses of his majesty. [17]For he received honor and glory from God the Father when the voice came to him from the Majestic Glory, saying, "This is my Son, whom I love; with him I am well pleased."[18]We ourselves heard this voice that came from heaven when we were with him on the sacred mountain.

> [19]*And we have the word of the prophets made more certain, and you will do well to pay attention to it, as to a light shining in a dark place, until the day dawns and the morning star rises in your hearts.* [20]*Above all, you must understand that no prophecy of Scripture came about by the prophet's own interpretation.* [21]*For prophecy never had its origin in the will of man, but men spoke from God as they were carried along by the Holy Spirit.*

An excellent example of the erosion of foundational doctrines being brought about by the ECM can be seen in discussions by emergent thinkers on the doctrine of the Atonement. It may surprise many within the evangelical community that there are actually several differing views about the purpose for and accomplishments of Christ's death on the cross. Throughout church history there have been many ideas brought forth to explain the atonement. Here is a short summary of the main theories:

The Ransom Theory – This is perhaps the earliest theory about the atonement. The theory states that by sinning in the garden, Adam and Eve made themselves (and by extension all of humanity) slaves to the devil. In order to redeem mankind, God provided His own Son's life as a ransom for mankind. In doing so, he actually tricked the devil because the devil did not realize that Christ could not be held by the bonds of death. Therefore, Christ's death on the cross paid the ransom for mankind, setting us free from bondage to the devil.

The Satisfaction Theory – In the 11th century, Anselm of Canterbury argued against the ransom view on the grounds that it was not Satan to whom a debt was owed, but rather God Himself because mankind had violated His decrees. In the Old Testament this debt was settled in part by the sacrificial system of the Jewish Temple. However, that was insufficient to fulfill the debt in whole. In response, God sent His Son, Jesus, who being both man and God (an infinite being) could pay the debt on our behalf to God the Father.

The Penal Substitution Theory – In the 16th century, the evangelical reformers built upon Anselm's satisfaction theory. The concern was that the satisfaction view looked more like a commercial transaction (payment for a debt) rather than a just penalty incurred as punishment for a transgression of the law. After all, the scriptures plainly state that the wages of sin is death. Therefore, the penal substitution view states that Jesus paid the penalty for our sins because we were unable to do so ourselves. Through His substitutionary sacrifice, both the righteousness and the justice of a holy God were satisfied completely. This is the theory that the evangelical community understands and accepts as the doctrine of the atonement today.

The Moral Example Theory – This more liberal theory, developed as a reaction to Anselm's satisfaction theory, holds that Christ died simply as an example to all mankind, provoking us toward living better, more fulfilled lives. This theory fits in very well with the concepts of living the way of Jesus and social justice that the ECM so strongly promotes. This theory suggests that the purpose of the atonement is neither about satisfying a debt nor about paying a penalty. Instead, it is about directing mankind to live the kind of deeply fulfilling life that God really wants us to live.

The 'Christus Victor' Theory – This is a modern reworking of the ransom theory, but in this theory Jesus does not act as a ransom used to purchase mankind back from the devil. Rather, this theory sees God and Satan locked in conflict over mankind, and Christ's death as allowing God to gain victory over Satan. Therefore the atonement is not really about saving mankind so much as it is about God defeating Satan through the work of Christ.

A high view of the authority and sufficiency of scripture clearly argues for the Penal Substitution theory of the atonement. However, by rejecting the authority of scripture and bringing into the discussion all of the various atonement theories, the ECM has created an atmosphere of confusion wherein all of the theories seem to make at least some kind of sense. Therefore, the emergent thinker would argue that since we cannot be certain as to what the absolute truth is, then all of the theories must contain aspects of it and all must be embraced equally. This even includes those theories that are obviously not supported by scripture.

How does this present itself in real life? Here are some examples of responses to the question of the atonement that were posted on Scot McKnight's web site, "Jesus Creed":

- *"I've never been able to take any one theory of the atonement and invest in it as the best explanation. They all have good aspects and offer something unique, but also*

> all end up feeling insufficient. A focus on one to the exclusion of the others can even lead to unhealthy expressions of faith."

- "But what we are talking about this morning is how we need to understand all views to see what is 'lacking' in ours. Thanks to theologians like [McKnight] who take the time to summarize them for us (as impartially as you can), 'hacks' like myself learn a lot... I'm with [another poster] and the 'mystic' in me. All have merit, none is complete. To settle on one is to settle for less than God."
- "I think it's more beautiful to embrace all than just one."[3]

I hope that you can see by the comments above how the thinking developed in the first river, postmodernism, and the practice developed in the second river, praxis, merge together in the river of the postevangelical. In them you can clearly see how the emergent thinker draws no distinction between a biblically accurate theory such as penal-substitution and one that has no biblical support such as the moral example theory. By equating the two, it is not so much that the non-biblical view is raised up to the level of Scripture. Instead it is Scripture that is brought down to the same level as all of the others.

Let me be very clear here that I am in no way suggesting that one needs to come to a full understanding the doctrine of the atonement in order to be saved. That is also true about many other foundational church doctrines, such as the trinity or the virgin birth. These doctrines don't provide the recipe for salvation to us, though the gospel would be incomplete without them. They exist in order to help us better understand who God is and how he interacts with mankind. But if we remove those

---

[3] Taken from Jesus Creed Blog (www.jesuscreed.org), posted on 2/17/2006, responses to 'Who tells the best atonement story', accessed 7/11/2007.

doctrinal foundations and say, "All that matters is that we believe in Jesus", we have created a shallow, unfruitful faith which in the end may not even be saving faith at all. Let me remind you that James tells us:

> **James 2:19:**
> [19]You believe that there is one God. Good! Even the demons believe that—and shudder.

A direct result of this obscuring of the foundational doctrines of our faith is further evident in the accusation of an "in versus out" attitude when it comes to personal salvation. The argument is that the traditional church, with specific reference to the evangelical community, draws far too fine a line in deciding who is "in", meaning saved, and those who are "out", meaning lost. By placing such hard boundaries around the reality of salvation, the evangelical church has created the kind of true/false propositional argument that the postmodern thinker finds so detestable. The emergent believer sees this kind of attitude as highly arrogant. After all, how can we know the true condition of a person's heart or the depth of their faith?

This ties back directly to the influence of the postmodern philosophy within the ECM. Recall that postmodernism seeks to be accepting of all ideas and philosophies <u>except</u> for those that claim to have an exclusive understanding of the truth. Here is a quote from an emerging church pastor named Bob Robinson which sums up well how the ECM feels about the in vs. out argument:

> "Exactly where do we draw the line around a set of doctrines that one must understand and believe in order for us to say, 'Yea, that person is now a follower of Jesus Christ.' And is it even wise to say that one must affirm a certain doctrinal belief structure in order to authentically have a relationship with Christ? ... But, and I ask this with great concern, what must a person affirm theologically before evangelical Christians would call that person a Christian? Can they be still learning to accept things like the Trinity or the Virgin Birth or even Penal Substitution? Or must they first articulate beliefs in these doctrines in order to be believers in Christ? In other words, when we say a Christian is a 'believer', do we mean that this person is a believer in sound doctrinal propositions or are we saying that they trust in the person of Jesus Christ?"[4]

It must be said that Robinson makes a good point and one to which the evangelical community would do well to listen. Many times, we in the evangelical church can become so concerned over whether a person's faith is genuine that we start to use doctrinal stances as a litmus test. We want to know what a person believes about the truths that are important to us or our own church family. If we find that we agree on these things, then we can let our guard down and enjoy a greater fellowship. If we don't agree, then we tend to raise our defenses and may even reject fellowship with that person because of differences over these core doctrines. But doctrinal knowledge is most certainly not the same thing as salvation. It will take time and learning before a new believer can grow to where they understand and relate those deeper truths properly.

---

[4] Taken from Vanguard Church Blog "JUMP – Velvet Jesus, Movement One" by Bob Robinson (vanguardchurch.blogspot.com/2007/04/jump-velvet-jesus-movement-one)

While the in vs. out argument does have merit in helping us to re-evaluate the ways in which we interact with others who claim to be followers of Christ, it does not change the fact that it was Jesus himself who affirmed an exclusive gospel. Here are just a few examples:

Matthew 7:13-14:

[13]"Enter through the narrow gate. For wide is the gate and broad is the road that leads to destruction, and many enter through it. [14]But small is the gate and narrow the road that leads to life, and only a few find it.

Matthew 7:21-23:

[21]"Not everyone who says to me, 'Lord, Lord,' will enter the kingdom of heaven, but only he who does the will of my Father who is in heaven. [22]Many will say to me on that day, 'Lord, Lord, did we not prophesy in your name, and in your name drive out demons and perform many miracles?' [23]Then I will tell them plainly, 'I never knew you. Away from me, you evildoers!'

John 14:6:

[6]Jesus answered, "I am the way and the truth and the life. No one comes to the Father except through me.

Buried within that quote by Robinson, there was also this statement:

"Granted, a person must meet the real Christ, not one made up and not one different than the person revealed on the pages of the Bible. And,

> *also granted, a person should have a legitimate desire to know the reality of God that is only revealed on the pages of the Bible"*[5]

This statement appears to bring the argument back around to one with which we would wholeheartedly agree, and affirms John 14:6. In order to be saved, one must place their faith in the one and only Jesus Christ, who is revealed to us through the pages of Scripture. But there are two difficulties with an emergent thinker making this statement. The first is that it is seemingly just a parenthetic addition to the main argument about in vs. out judgments. In other words it is not really as important as the argument itself. And the second is that this statement creates the kind of exclusive proposition from which postmodernism desperately wants to distance itself. To say that the Bible is *the* source of revelation about God is to make the Bible the *exclusive* provider of a knowable and understandable truth.

But the in vs. out argument is not really about the authority of scripture, it is about our own ability to understand when a person becomes a member of the family of God. In the end it is an assault on the Gospel itself. Because emergent thinkers argue that we cannot truly know who is saved and who is not, they contend that we should give the benefit of the doubt to all. In other words, we should assume that all people who don't outright reject God are either in the church or are moving toward it, one day to become part of it. If that is the case, then we don't need to confront people with the reality of the gospel, but rather help them along the path toward discovering the truth for themselves. This creates an open gospel

---
[5] Ibid

that is accepting of all ideals because, after all, in the end everyone is basically heading in the same direction. That is, unless they make a conscious and absolute decision to reject Christ.

In keeping along with the 'post' idea, McKnight concludes that the ECM is post bible study piety. People within the ECM are very concerned that the world does not see them as a bunch of "Bible thumping Christians". They feel that the traditional church has created an environment where biblical knowledge is more important than compassion for the poor and the lost. This challenge is driven by the idea that what one does is more important than what one believes, as well as by their focus on social justice. The ECM does raise a valid concern here, and one which the apostle Paul addresses in 1st Corinthians 13:

> **_1 Corinthians 13:1-3:_**
> *¹If I speak in the tongues of men and of angels, but have not love, I am only a resounding gong or a clanging cymbal. ²If I have the gift of prophecy and can fathom all mysteries and all knowledge, and if I have a faith that can move mountains, but have not love, I am nothing. ³If I give all I possess to the poor and surrender my body to the flames, but have not love, I gain nothing.*

However correct the emergent might be in raising the concern of placing knowledge over love and compassion, the answer is not to simply forego the study of scripture for the sake of appearing to be more compassionate. It is just the contrary. If one does study the scripture honestly and thoroughly then one should come to the same conclusions as Paul. Let us not forget that Paul was one of the most educated men in the early church. He spent the early years of his life as the prize student of Gamaliel, who was the teacher of teachers among the Pharisees of his day. And it was through his knowledge of the Old Testament and his understanding of what would eventually become the New Testament, that he saw knowledge without love and compassion was meaningless.

The answer does not lie with less bible study but rather with more and deeper bible study. To reject the study of scripture and replace it with the acceptance of a consensus of ideas is completely contrary to what God tells us in 2 Timothy:

> **2 Timothy 3:14-17:**
>
> [14]But as for you, continue in what you have learned and have become convinced of, because you know those from whom you learned it, [15]and how from infancy you have known the holy Scriptures, which are able to make you wise for salvation through faith in Christ Jesus. [16]All Scripture is God-breathed and is useful for teaching, rebuking, correcting and training in righteousness, [17]so that the man of God may be thoroughly equipped for every good work.

A further aspect of being post-bible study piety is the rejection of systematic theology. Systematic theology really saw its fruition during the modern era, and represents a logical, step by step format within which to know and experience God. The ECM rejects this for several reasons. First, because they are looking for a consensus opinion about an issue and a systematic theology does not lend itself to that end. A systematic understanding of Gods revelation will quite naturally be propositional in nature, meaning that it leads to concrete opinions of right and wrong. This of course goes hard against the grain of the postmodern mindset, and so it is quickly rejected as being exclusionary.

A second problem raised with the reliance upon a systematic theology is the argument that God, through the Bible, did not give us an academic textbook. Rather, He gave us a storied narrative. The purpose of this narrative is to demonstrate how God interacts with mankind, and teach us how to improve our own interactions with Him. A further assertion is that there are many truths that exist outside of the scriptures, therefore the Bible cannot be the only source of revelation. For example, the Bible does not teach anything about the structure of molecules or atoms, yet we know for a fact that they do indeed exist. The argument contends that since there are truths that exist outside of the Bible, then the Bible must be only one of many sources of revelation from God. If the Bible is just one of many storybooks through which God is attempting to reveal himself, then of course one cannot base their faith solely on a systematic study of that singular text. But if the Bible is sufficient, complete, and authoritative concerning spiritual truth, then it is *the* source of *the* truth that must be understood through an intensive study of what it reveals.

A final concern that is raised by many in the ECM on this issue of theology is an argument regarding languages. The emergent would say that no one language is capable of conveying all of the wonderful expressions about who God is. They would point to the difficulty of translating the scriptures from the original languages into our own to show that we simply cannot, of ourselves, understand enough to say that we know what the revealed truth is. Therefore, they assert, it is better to accept it as a mystery rather than waste time in vain attempts to learn that which is inherently unknowable. Rob Bell and his wife related this concept clearly in an interview with *Christianity Today* in November, 2004:

> *The Bells started questioning their assumptions about the Bible itself – "discovering the Bible as human product" as Rob puts it, rather than the product of divine fiat. "The Bible is still in the center for us," Rob says, "but it's a different kind of center. We want to embrace mystery rather than conquer it."*
>
> *"I grew up thinking that we've figured out the Bible," Kristen says, "that we knew what it means. Now I have no idea what most of it means. And yet I feel like life is big again – like life used to be black and white, and now it's in color"*[6]

This line of thinking ultimately leads down a pathway of doubt and uncertainty. Yes, it is true that any structured format of trying to understand God will have problems. After all, it is finite humankind, with our capacity for understanding darkened by the fall, trying to comprehend an infinite God. But if God himself commands us to seek Him in order that we might know Him, and tells us that the Bible is His Word revealed to us, then it is nothing short of disobedience (i.e.: rebellion) to simply push that understanding aside with a label that reads "mystery". If we cease trying to understand God is an orderly way, then we set ourselves adrift without any kind of anchor, and we'll never really know if we are going in the right direction or not. As Brian McLaren puts it:

---

[6] Andy Crouch, "The Emergent Mystique," *Christianity Today*, November 2004, pg 37-38

> *Sit down here next to me in this little restaurant and ask me if Christianity (my version of it, yours, the Pope's, whoever's) is orthodox, meaning true, and here's my honest answer: a little, but not yet. Assuming by Christianity you mean the Christian understanding of the world and God, Christian opinions on soul, text, and culture... I'd have to say we probably have a couple of things right, but a lot of things wrong.*[7]
>
> *Ultimately, I hope that Jesus will save Buddhism, Islam and every other religion, including the Christian religion, which often seems to need saving about as much as any other religion does. (In the context, I do wish all Christians would become followers of Jesus, but perhaps this is too much to ask. After all, I'm not doing such a hot job of it myself.)*[8]

A postmodern viewpoint forces the ECM to reject the singular authority of scripture. That casts mankind adrift in an endless sea of religious ideas and philosophies – a few of them true, many more false. Taken at face value, one would have to read McLaren's words and ask "How can anyone ever hope to know God?" The emergent would say that thinking one can know God is an arrogant thought in and of itself. Thankfully though, we have a God who seeks after us, who not only wants us to know Him, but who also provides a way to do so - the Holy Scriptures:

> **Romans 16:25-27:**
> [25] Now to him who is able to establish you by my gospel and the proclamation of Jesus Christ, according to the revelation of the mystery hidden for long ages past, [26] but now revealed and made known through the prophetic writings by the command of the eternal God, so that all

---

[7] Brian McLaren, A Generous Orthodoxy (Grand Rapids: Zondervan, 2004)pg 293
[8] Ibid., pg 264

nations might believe and obey him— ²⁷*to the only wise God be glory forever through Jesus Christ! Amen.*

Chapter 7

<u>John 6:26:</u>

²⁶Jesus answered, "I tell you the truth, you are looking for me, not because you saw miraculous signs but because you ate the loaves and had your fill.

The Fourth River: Political

The fourth and final river in Scot McKnight's metaphor for the emerging church he calls simply, Political. While the ECM is not a formal organization which could be considered a political force, its individual members have a very active interest in the political scene. That is not to say that the ECM is looking to stage some sort of coup within the traditional church. What it means is that those involved in the ECM unashamedly mix their political viewpoints with their faith. In some cases, particularly within the Emergent group, those political ideals are given an equal weight with scripture itself and serve to direct the churches in forming their belief systems and guiding their activities.

An important disclaimer is required at this point. Just as in most other aspects of the ECM, there is a broad spectrum as to the degree of political orientation and activity within the various churches. As a general rule, the more liberal the stance of the individual church, the more politically active the climate for that congregation. Emerging churches that would be considered more conservative in nature (i.e.: Carson's confessional camp or Driscoll's contemporary worship form) will place far less importance on political ideology than those on the other end of the spectrum, who have fully embraced postmodernism (Carson's heterodox or Driscoll's emergent groups). Most of the writing that is done on behalf of the ECM appears to come out of the more liberal Emergent group, and as a result the political leaning of the ECM tends to be heavily weighted toward the liberal versus conservative side of the spectrum.

The political argument that tends to resonate most from the ECM is that the traditional church sees all politics in terms of only two issues: abortion and prayer in schools. The complaint is that the traditional church, with particular emphasis on the evangelical church, focuses so much on those two issues that they are completely blind to the myriad of other political and social issues that they believe should concern us all. The ECM wants the church to see other political issues as every bit as important as abortion or prayer. These would include poverty, equal rights (ethnic as well as gay rights), feminism, and environmentalism.

The political focus for the ECM flows from the concept of Social Justice, which we looked at in the previous chapter. Because the ECM has so openly embraced the concept of social justice, it has become a major attraction for outside groups which are active politically in that arena – many of them with openly liberal agendas. At the same time, the intentional lack of a clearly defined doctrinal structure has made it possible for many within those outside groups to become deeply involved with the ECM, even when their personal lifestyles are unmistakably rejected by scripture. A clear example of this is the strong presence of the gay rights community within the Emergent group. Therefore, the root of the political impulse of the ECM appears to lie in the promotion of social change through religious or spiritual influence.

Many outside the church and within the ECM would argue that in many instances, the modern evangelical church has placed too much emphasis on soul winning and not nearly enough on ministering to those who are in need. I myself have visited churches where the altar call was almost as long as the sermon itself and yet those same churches had very little to give to ministries geared toward those outside of the congregation. This was especially true if the ministry would not immediately lead to a significant number of conversions. It is much easier to simply say, "Jesus is the answer to your problems" and then move on to the next person rather than try and minister to people even when they reject the gospel. These ministries seem to have placed all of their emphasis on getting people saved and then leaving it up to God find some another way to fix their other problems. I'm doing a little equal-opportunity stereotyping here, but I hope you understand my point. By looking only to the evangelistic needs of our world, many churches have left a vacuum that has been readily filled by other groups which have little or no care about true spiritual needs. Yet these organizations are more than willing to look after the physical needs of their neighbors and fulfill the role of the good samaritan.

It is largely because of this one-sided emphasis on the part of the evangelical church that the social gospel has made such inroads into the ECM. Recall that the idea behind social justice is seeking to correct physical injustices that exist within our world. The most widespread problem to be addressed is that of poverty. The social gospel advances the idea that it is the responsibility of the church not only to care for the poor, but to actively seek to eliminate poverty altogether. Yet even Christ Himself did not seek to accomplish this. Consider the story of the feeding of the five thousand in John chapter 6 and the results of that event. The miracle which occurred was great, and as a result there were many who sought to follow after Jesus. But the reason they sought to follow Him was because they got their bellies filled – not because they saw Him as their true Messiah. Jesus Himself rebuked them for this:

> **John 6:26-27:**
> [26] Jesus answered, "I tell you the truth, you are looking for me, not because you saw miraculous signs but because you ate the loaves and had your fill. [27] Do not work for food that spoils, but for food that endures to eternal life, which the Son of Man will give you. On him God the Father has placed his seal of approval."

As we saw in the Postevangelical river, the Emergent's response to the evangelical church is to reject the gospel as we know it and replace it with a social ministry, or living the way of Jesus. In doing so, they open the door to a political agenda which seeks to effect social change by means of political power. There are many outspoken proponents of the social gospel who are not officially affiliated with the ECM, so it is not the movement's own personal agenda that is being promoted. However, what the social gospel is seeking to accomplish is widely embraced by leaders within the ECM, and so they readily provide those outside the movement with a base from which to expand their influence.

Without question, God has charged the church the responsibility of ministering to those who are in need; but we must also keep our focus first and foremost on the great commission – to go and make disciples, not to go and eliminate homelessness and hunger. As is the case with so many other things, there is a balance that needs to be established. But in adopting the goals of the social gospel, Emergent leaders have opened themselves up to a political force that has eagerly joined itself to their movement for the sake of enhancing its own exposure, credibility and power.

Another aspect of the political focus of the ECM, again with emphasis on the Emergent group, is that of gay rights and the acceptance of homosexuality into the church. This focus is made possible by the rejection of the Bible as the highest authority and source of truth. We know that the movement's reliance on postmodern thinking has led to a view that the scriptures are not the final arbiter of truth. The Emergent thinker believes that there are many subtle complexities to any topic that must first be explored and understood before making any determinations of right or wrong. This is exactly what has occurred regarding the topic of homosexuality.

In January of 2006, Brian McLaren presented an article in Leadership Journal which was later presented on the journal's web site, known as "Out of Ur". In that article, he wrote about being questioned by visitors to his church as to where he stood on the topic of homosexuality. His observations about the topic, and how he believes the church should respond to it, brought forth a very strong response from the readers and showed quite clearly the problems that are created when one applies postmodern thinking to Biblical truth.

McLaren begins his article with the following thought:

> "I hesitate in answering 'the homosexual question' not because I'm a cowardly flip-flopper who wants to tickle ears, but because I am a pastor, and pastors have learned from Jesus that there is more to answering a question than being right or even honest: we must also be...pastoral."[9]

He then goes on to say:

> "Frankly, many of us don't know what we should think about homosexuality. We've heard all sides but no position has yet won our confidence so that we can say 'it seems good to the Holy Spirit and us.'"[10]

What McLaren does (and many Emergent thinkers with him), is to openly consider the legitimacy of the homosexual lifestyle within the church, because in our modern day it is becoming so widely accepted. This

---

[9] Brian McLaren on the Homosexual Question: Finding a Pastoral Response; http://blog.christianitytoday.com/outofur/archives/2006/01/brian_mclaren_o.html; accessed 6/13/2008.
[10] Ibid

is done even in spite of scriptures that clearly define such a lifestyle as an abomination and a sin. What could cause a Christian to even entertain such thinking? It is because the Emergent believer no longer sees the Bible as the sole governing authority, but instead one that must be interpreted along with other authorities in light of current circumstances. Remember Rob Bell's statement:

> *"So if we are serious about following God, then we have to interpret the Bible. It is not possible to simply do what the Bible says. We must first make decisions about what it means at this time, in this place, for these people."*[11]

When the Emergent believer makes the interpretation of biblical texts dependent upon current social trends, they make the Bible the slave of a social democratic rule. This is an open invitation to any political group that wishes to justify their position by means of the church and its membership.

As one might imagine, McLaren's article elicited a strong critical response from the conservative church. In defending his apparent disregard of the scriptural condemnation of homosexuality, McLaren wrote the following:

> *"Please be assured that as a pastor and as someone who loves and seeks to follow the Bible, I am aware of Genesis 19, Leviticus 18:22 and 20:13, Romans 1, 1 Corinthians 6:9, and related texts. Believe me, I have read them and prayerfully pondered them, and have read extensively on*

---

[11] Rob Bell, *Velvet Elvis: Repainting the Christian Faith* (Grand Rapids, Zondervan) pg 46

all the many sides of the issue. I understand that for many people, these verses end all dialogue and people like me must seem horribly stupid not to see what's there so clearly to them. I wish they could understand that some of us encounter additional levels of complexity when we try honestly and faithfully to face these texts... On a deeper level, some of us feel we are being dishonest and unfaithful to Scripture unless we face questions about how we should interpret and apply these texts today, and what hermeneutical methods and assumptions underlie our interpretations and applications."[12]

This open interpretation of the Bible is what leads McLaren to his position on the legitimacy of the homosexual relationship and how God's church should respond to it:

"Even if we are convinced that all homosexual behavior is always sinful, we still want to treat gay and lesbian people with more dignity, gentleness, and respect than our colleagues do. If we think that there may actually be a legitimate context for some homosexual relationships, we know that the biblical arguments are nuanced and multilayered, and the pastoral ramifications are staggeringly complex. We aren't sure if or where lines are to be drawn, nor do we know how to enforce with fairness whatever lines are drawn.

Perhaps we need a five-year moratorium on making pronouncements. In the meantime, we'll practice prayerful Christian dialogue, listening respectfully, disagreeing agreeably. When decisions need to be made, they'll be admittedly provisional. We'll keep our ears attuned to scholars in biblical studies, theology, ethics, psychology, genetics, sociology, and related fields. Then in five years, if we have

---

[12] Brian McLaren on the Homosexual Question 4: McLaren's Response; http://blog.christianitytoday.com/outofur/archives/2006/01/brian_mclaren_o_3.html, accessed 6/13/2008

> clarity, we'll speak; if not, we'll set another five years for ongoing reflection. After all, many important issues in church history took centuries to figure out. Maybe this moratorium would help us resist the "winds of doctrine" blowing furiously from the left and right, so we can patiently wait for the wind of the Spirit to set our course."[13]

To be fair, I don't believe that McLaren is trying to be overtly political in his assessment. But the position that he takes is not to take any stand at all, and that is an open invitation for politically motivated activity to enter into the church. The Bible teaches very clearly that homosexuality is sin, just like adultery or any other sexually immoral act. If a church leader stands up and declares that we just don't know if it is right or wrong, then those on the side of the gay rights movement will quickly seek to join with that leader in an effort to bring legitimacy to their particular position. And this is how a political agenda suddenly becomes part of the framework of the Emerging Church Movement.

When he writes about the political leanings of the ECM in this fourth river, Scot Mcknight makes the following observation:

> "And though emerging leaders often speak of the bi-partisan or non-partisan nature of emergent, I don't see it. I think they are mostly politically left. Brian McLaren called for a 'purple' politics. I'll believe the emerging movement is 'purple' in politics when I see a politics that is genuinely moderate, genuinely independent...The purple politics spoken of in the emerging movement is nothing but Democratic partisan

---

[13] Brian McLaren on the Homosexual Question: Finding a Pastoral Response; http://blog.christianitytoday.com/outofur/archives/2006/01/brian_mclaren_o.html; accessed 6/13/2008.

> *cabbages dressed up in enough rhetoric to look like an independent cauliflower. It isn't.*"[14]

It is not surprising that political influences are a major aspect of the ECM when one considers the backgrounds of both the leadership and members. Most are young, well educated and socially active. They grew up within an educational system that promoted postmodernism as well as social responsibility, and in which liberal social activism is seen as a noble cause. This is not an attempt to denigrate these people in any way. It simply helps to understand that a group whose educational and social background celebrates political activism would most certainly welcome it into their church life.

While it may be true that the ECM did not set out to become a political entity, the very nature of its members and their belief systems have led it to become heavily involved in the political scene. Their focus on social justice, as well as proactive study of alternative belief systems, has become an open invitation to liberal political groups. The postmodern philosophy tells us that we are all intellectually constrained by our backgrounds and that we must look beyond ourselves in order to gain a clear perspective of what the truth might be. It is ironic then that Emergent believers have so readily adopted such biased political views into their churches. In the end, they run the very real risk of having their direction dictated by politicians rather than what God teaches.

---

[14] Scot McKnight, *What is the Emerging Church?* (Fall Contemporary Issues Conference, Westminster Theological Seminary) October 2006, Pgs. 27-28

Chapter 8

<u>Philippians 1:9-11:</u>

⁹And this is my prayer: that your love may abound more and more in knowledge and depth of insight, ¹⁰so that you may be able to discern what is best and may be pure and blameless until the day of Christ, ¹¹filled with the fruit of righteousness that comes through Jesus Christ—to the glory and praise of God.

A Proper Response

Dr. Scot McKnight, in describing his view of the ECM from an insider's perspective, uses the metaphor of a lake which has four rivers leading into it. Having looked at the four rivers individually, it is now only fitting for us to take a step back and see if we can make some sense of how they all fit together, and how we should respond. Just as a review, the four rivers are: Postmodernism, Praxis, Postevangelical, and Political. These four rivers and their ultimate destination, Lake Emergent, represent quite a spectrum of beliefs from mainstream conservative to postmodern liberal, and they serve to remind us just how complicated it can be to try and place labels upon the participants within the ECM. In keeping with the metaphor, one can see that each river has its own source and its own unique characteristics. Each one may have a different level of appeal for those who wish to travel upon it. But as one draws closer to Lake Emergent while moving along those rivers, they begin to merge together becoming more theologically liberal and postmodern oriented. The final stopping point, Lake Emergent, is the residence of those who have fully adopted postmodern thinking into their faith. As such, the lake itself represents the most liberal thinkers and churches within the whole of the ECM.

Having seen all of the complexities of trying to understand a movement like the ECM, we must now decide how or even if we should interact with this new movement within our churches. Should we welcome this new movement? Should we condemn it? Can we afford to ignore it? The sheer scope of the movement means that we cannot ignore it, so the choice comes down to whether or not we can welcome it into our churches and if so, to what degree.

Postmodern thinkers call upon us to exercise a proper confidence in our approach to making decisions. By that, they mean to say that we must first admit our own shortcomings and inability to grasp every nuance of the truth that is involved. They would ask us to withhold bold claims of fact and by all means avoid exclusive statements about certainty and the truth. The Bible, however, calls us to a different type of confidence – a confidence that the word of God is the truth, and that we can fully rely upon it to guide us in our decisions. Based upon that confidence and the clear teaching of the scriptures, I would offer the following as a proper response to the Emerging Church Movement.

First and foremost, both as the church and as individuals we must be focused on fulfilling our calling in Christ, and that means we must focus on the gospel. The problem for the Emerging Church is that they feel the gospel of the Bible is too sharp, too harsh. The Bible presents a gospel that is highly propositional and clearly divisive, and that is what God intended. Postmodern thinkers wish to try and temper that harsh edge in order to make it more palatable for the outside world. In so doing, the liberal side of the ECM offers up many alternative gospels which stand in contrast to that which is clearly presented in scripture. There is a right and a wrong, a good and a bad, and we human beings must face the divide between a holy, righteous God and our sinful selves.

The gospel of our Lord is exclusive. The Bible clearly tells us, speaking of Jesus:

> *Acts 4:12:*
> *"Salvation is found in no one else, for there is no other name under heaven given to men by which we must be saved."*

And any attempt to broaden the gospel or make it more accommodating of other beliefs is a direct contradiction to the words of Jesus Himself:

> *Matthew 7:13:*
> *[13]"Enter through the narrow gate. For wide is the gate and broad is the road that leads to destruction, and many enter through it. [14]But small is the gate and narrow the road that leads to life, and only a few find it."*

A focus on the gospel should in no way end just because a person has been saved. Rather, that is to be just the beginning of a life whose central theme revolves around God's truth. The real power of the gospel does not lie simply in the ability to have our sins forgiven. Rather, it is in the restoration of our relationship with Almighty God, the Creator and Sustainer of all things. It does not just provide a means of escape from eternal punishment; it also grants to us adoption into the family of the King Himself. And not only that, it works in us every day to transform us into the very image of Christ.

One of the main problems that I see with the ECM is that their definition of the gospel is often somewhat vague. I have read ECM authors who use the term interchangeably at times to refer to the gospel of Christ (by which we are saved), as well as the social gospel (through which social justice is carried out), and sometimes to nothing more than a move toward a spiritual awakening. While they may see these as just different aspects of the same thing, I cannot agree with that position. The definition of the gospel that is spelled out in the scriptures is that it is the good news of Christ – that though we were sinners and separated from God, Jesus (God Incarnate) came to earth, lived a sinless life, died on the cross to pay the price for our sins, and rose again in triumph so that we might know God and live with Him for the remainder of eternity. Any other good thing that takes place in my life is an outworking of that gospel, but it is not the gospel. If I care for the poor, it honors God because it reflects His mercy and grace, but it is not the gospel. If I care for the environment, it reflects His love for His creation, but it is not the gospel. When I conduct business, I do so in a way that honors God through honesty and fairness, but that is not the gospel. Those are all good things and right for us to do, but those acts are not the gospel itself, they are the fruit that is brought about as a result of it.

In his book, *A New Kind of Christian*, Brian McLaren writes:

> *"Look, my understanding of the gospel tells me that religion is always a mixed bag, whether it's Judaism, Christianity, Islam, or Buddhism. ...But isn't that the point of the gospel – that we're all a mess, whatever our religion, in need of God's grace??"*[1]

In a way, McLaren is pointing out one aspect of the gospel; that it is the means by which we receive God's saving grace. But what he misses is that it is not the gospel which demonstrates our need for a savior; that is the purpose of the law. It is the law that shows us our inability to meet God's requirements on our own, and thereby our need for His grace. It is through the gospel that His grace is given to us. Neither does the gospel belong to Judaism or Islam or Buddhism, or any other religious system - it is exclusively Christian. It is not to help other religions grow closer to God within their own faith systems. Instead, it calls people away from their wrong beliefs to the truth and to a relationship with the one true God. And this is done on God's terms, not theirs. McLaren appears to go so far as to say that the gospel is greater than mere religion, but stops short of accepting it as the exclusive truth of God that it is.

---

[1] McLaren, Brian, *A New Kind of Christian: A Tale of Two Friends on a Spiritual Journey* (San Francisco, Jossey-Bass) pg 66

The Bible defines the truth of the gospel in quite specific terms. We cannot know the absolute condition of a person's heart, so therefore we cannot say without a doubt who is or is not saved (who is in or who is out). However, the gospel spells out for us specifically what is required for salvation, and also how that will lead to a God centered life as we are sanctified to be like Christ. If a person rejects the requirements spelled out by the gospel (repentance from sin, faith in Christ alone, etc.), then that person has rejected God's terms and has placed themselves firmly in the 'out' category. If a person tries to substitute good works or even 'living the way of Jesus' for faith, then they will still find themselves in the 'out' category. The same is also true for those who might try to add a belief in Jesus to their own religious system. We can never back down from the exclusivity of the gospel of Christ or try to soften it so as to make it more palatable for those who are lost. Remember:

I Corinthians 1:18
For the message of the cross is foolishness to those who are perishing, but to us who are being saved it is the power of God.

Romans 1:16
I am not ashamed of the gospel, because it is the power of God for the salvation of everyone who believes: first for the Jew, then for the Gentile.

While our primary response as the body of Christ should be to focus on the gospel, it is every bit as important that we stand firm on the Word of God. The Bible is the foundational revelation from God to mankind. If we remove that foundation or even simply chip away at parts of it, then we have lost the anchor upon which our faith stands. If we weaken the scriptures, we have built our house upon the sand and not upon the rock. When the storms come, that religious house built upon the sand will surely fall.

The world will always be happy to provide an alternative to the exclusive truth of the scriptures. That is after all where the fall of man began, and it remains the enemy's tactic even to this day. Even in the end, his goal will be to create an impersonation of Christ, the anti-Christ, in order to lead the world away from God. The church must therefore stand firm upon the inspiration, sufficiency, and inerrancy of the scriptures.

Emergent thinkers assert that we must understand how the scriptures apply to us in light of our evolving culture. However scripture itself argues that we should never try to interpret the meaning of a passage based upon what is happening to us today. Instead, we should seek to understand what the author (both divine and human) meant as it was written. Then we should try to understand how that truth applies to us in our present circumstances. It is the truth that guides our actions, not the other way around. To do otherwise is to impose our own will upon the teaching, and that will lead us inevitably to false doctrines. The truth of God's word must guide us, not some form of spiritual democracy which seeks to justify whatever direction our society takes, and then looks for ways to rationalize the biblical teachings. A couple of passages come to mind that should never become commonplace where this is concerned:

> ***2 Peter 1:20, 21:***
>
> [20]*Above all, you must understand that no prophecy of Scripture came about by the prophet's own interpretation.* [21]*For prophecy never had its origin in the will of man, but men spoke from God as they were carried along by the Holy Spirit.*
>
> ***2 Timothy 3:16-17***
>
> [16]*All Scripture is God-breathed and is useful for teaching, rebuking, correcting and training in righteousness,* [17]*so that the man of God may be thoroughly equipped for every good work.*

If we look back at the formation of the early church in the book of Acts, we can see that they too had to deal with changes within the church and the culture surrounding it. The new church that had grown in Jerusalem had seen its own share of ups and downs. After Christ's resurrection and subsequent ascension into heaven, the church had seen the miracles of Pentecost, an exponential growth rate (which presented its own problems), and the creation of a more formalized structure. Yet along with the miracles came great oppression – especially at the hands of the Jewish leadership. This persecution forced the church out of Jerusalem and into other communities in the region. It was during this time that congregations in cities outside of Jerusalem began to appear. One such congregation was the church in Antioch:

> ***Acts 11: 19-26:***
>
> [19]*Now those who had been scattered by the persecution in connection with Stephen traveled as far as Phoenicia, Cyprus and Antioch,*

> telling the message only to Jews. ²⁰Some of them, however, men from Cyprus and Cyrene, went to Antioch and began to speak to Greeks also, telling them the good news about the Lord Jesus. ²¹The Lord's hand was with them, and a great number of people believed and turned to the Lord.
>
> ²²News of this reached the ears of the church at Jerusalem, and they sent Barnabas to Antioch. ²³When he arrived and saw the evidence of the grace of God, he was glad and encouraged them all to remain true to the Lord with all their hearts. ²⁴He was a good man, full of the Holy Spirit and faith, and a great number of people were brought to the Lord.
>
> ²⁵Then Barnabas went to Tarsus to look for Saul, ²⁶and when he found him, he brought him to Antioch. So for a whole year Barnabas and Saul met with the church and taught great numbers of people. The disciples were called Christians first at Antioch.

Antioch was not a Jewish city, and Acts 11:20 tells us that this new congregation was formed when those who had left Jerusalem began to preach the gospel to the Greek population there. Word of this new group soon reached back to Jerusalem, and it can be inferred from the passage in Acts that there was some concern as to whether or not this group of believers was indeed part of the new church, or was just some other religious sect that had sprouted up. In order to find out exactly what was happening, the church leaders in Jerusalem dispatched Barnabas to go and check things out first hand.

Barnabas traveled to Antioch, and what he discovered is described as "evidence of the grace of God". In other words, he saw that what was growing there was indeed the same faith that Jesus had imparted to the believers in Jerusalem. I'm quite certain that there were differences in the way these groups went about worshipping, and certainly their backgrounds were worlds apart (Jewish culture versus Greek culture). And yet, God's work was going forward in that place. Barnabas' response to all of this was first to encourage them (verse 23), and then to begin teaching them (verse 26). The result of his ministry there was that a great many were saved and the church there in Antioch grew.

Barnabas also saw the need for a long-term relationship with that church. He knew that they would need to be taught the fundamentals of the Christian faith, the roots of which were found in the teaching of the Jews. So Barnabas went to look for a man who was arguably the number one scholar within the church (and also the man who would pen the majority of the New Testament). That man was Paul, who was still known as Saul at that time. Barnabas went out, found Paul, and brought him to Antioch to begin teaching the believers there the truths and doctrines of the scriptures. The passage tells us that Paul and Barnabas spent an entire year there teaching the new believers the truths of the gospel. As a result, the church in Antioch grew to such a level that they made a name for themselves – Christians. It would certainly seem to me that if we wanted a model of how we should react to any new movement within the church, this would be it!

Looking over that passage of scripture, one can see three key elements that were put into action. They are discernment, encouragement, and mutual edification. As we determine how to respond to the Emerging

Church Movement, we would do well to put these same elements to work ourselves.

Discernment

Discernment is the ability to tell the difference between what is good and bad, right and wrong. Discernment was required on the part of the early church leaders when they looked at what was transpiring around them. Already there were teachers who were spreading false doctrines among the believers. The early church leaders had to be certain that wherever a body of believers grew up, and claimed to be part of what Jesus had established, that they really were part of the Body of Christ. Therefore, when this new group began to grow in Antioch, the Jerusalem leaders sent one of their best, Barnabas, to observe and discern if they truly were part of the Body of Christ.

Discernment is required of us as well as we focus on the ECM because the Bible clearly tells us:

> ***2 Timothy 4:3-4***
> [3] *For the time will come when men will not put up with sound doctrine. Instead, to suit their own desires, they will gather around them a great number of teachers to say what their itching ears want to hear.* [4] *They will turn their ears away from the truth and turn aside to myths.*

1 Timothy 6:3-5

³*If anyone teaches false doctrines and does not agree to the sound instruction of our Lord Jesus Christ and to godly teaching, ⁴he is conceited and understands nothing. He has an unhealthy interest in controversies and quarrels about words that result in envy, strife, malicious talk, evil suspicions ⁵and constant friction between men of corrupt mind, who have been robbed of the truth and who think that godliness is a means to financial gain.*

The acceptance of the postmodern philosophy into the belief system of the Emergent has unfortunately led many of their leaders to become the very ones that God warns us about in those passages. Yet there are others within the movement who have not adopted those beliefs as their own, and remain steadfastly committed to the truths of the scriptures. Our calling is to discern who is teaching the truth and who is not, and not to simply dismiss them all out of hand. What this requires is that we take steps to educate ourselves so that we can tell the difference. That means we must spend time in God's Word; reading, learning, even memorizing so that we have the knowledge we need when the time for discernment comes.

Barnabas was not just a fringe member of the church in Jerusalem. He was already established as a teacher within the church, one who knew the scriptures well. Recall also that it was Barnabas that brought Saul to the apostles after seeing that he truly had been changed, and was now a follower of Christ. That may be exactly why he was their choice to go and observe what was happening in Antioch – he had both the knowledge of

God's word and wisdom to put it to use. The apostle Paul reinforced this same idea for us when he wrote:

> ### 2 Timothy 3:14-15
>
> ^{14}But as for you, continue in what you have learned and have become convinced of, because you know those from whom you learned it, ^{15}and how from infancy you have known the holy Scriptures, which are able to make you wise for salvation through faith in Christ Jesus.
>
> ### 1 Timothy 3:13-16
>
> ^{13}Until I come, devote yourself to the public reading of Scripture, to preaching and to teaching. ^{14}Do not neglect your gift, which was given you through a prophetic message when the body of elders laid their hands on you.
>
> ^{15}Be diligent in these matters; give yourself wholly to them, so that everyone may see your progress. ^{16}Watch your life and doctrine closely. Persevere in them, because if you do, you will save both yourself and your hearers.
>
> ### 2 Timothy 2:15
>
> ^{15}Do your best to present yourself to God as one approved, a workman who does not need to be ashamed and who correctly handles the word of truth.

The key to discernment is not only knowing what you believe, but why you believe it. This means moving beyond adopting a belief just because it sounds good or someone you know and admire believes it. It means digging into the scriptures yourself to see if what is being taught is true, just as the Bereans did:

Acts 17:11

¹¹*Now the Bereans were of more noble character than the Thessalonians, for they received the message with great eagerness and examined the Scriptures every day to see if what Paul said was true.*

Please note that I am not talking about becoming legalistic or dividing over what can be called issues of reason. Examples of that might be the argument over live versus recorded music, which version of the Bible to use, formal versus casual attire in church, or even which color of carpet to have in the sanctuary. Paul addressed this topic very thoroughly in 1st Corinthians chapter 8. What I am speaking about is learning and truly understanding what the Bible teaches as the truth, so that we can stand against the false teachings of those who would try to dissuade us from that truth. Our charge is to know God's Word in such a way that we can tell the difference.

Encouragement

After Barnabas arrived in Antioch and saw that what was taking place was indeed of God, he set out to encourage those believers. Notice that it does not say that Barnabas encouraged them to act like the church in Jerusalem, or to send representatives there in order to learn the right way to go about building their church, or even which programs to put in place. He simply began by encouraging them to set as their first and highest priority that of remaining true to God.

Not everyone goes about performing the ministry of the church in exactly the same way. I may like a more traditional service while you might enjoy a more contemporary or blended service. Our church might have an on-campus Sunday school program while another might use small groups that meet away from the church building sometime during the week. But so long as our focus is the same, that being the gospel and the scriptures, then the method should not become a matter for division. Diversity is also a part of God's creation, and should not be excluded from His church. In saying this I'm not advocating trying to act like the world in order to attract the world - not by any means. The church should look different from the world because we are different. But we should not disparage others simply because they choose a different format within which to minister. To believe that every church has to look exactly like our own leads us down the same terrible, legalistic path that the Pharisees trod so long ago.

My concern here is that there are those within the Emerging Church community that are still holding true to God's Word, but who are being shunned simply because of the type of ministry in which they are involved. These people should not be turned out simply because they are seeking ways to reach the postmodern community. To do so is just as damaging as accepting false doctrines into our own church body. Instead, these brothers and sisters in Christ should be encouraged to pursue their outreach with the support of the mainstream church (this, of course, assumes that they remain faithful to both the gospel and the scriptures). We should actively seek to encourage Christians who are reaching a group that would never otherwise be seen by most of us, so that they can reach them with the real truth. To do otherwise condemns the lost to receive only the false teachings that will guide them down the path to destruction. If we don't teach them the truth, the world most certainly will not.

Mutual Edification

Romans 14:19
Let us therefore make every effort to do what leads to peace and to mutual edification.

2 Timothy 4:2
²Preach the Word; be prepared in season and out of season; correct, rebuke and encourage—with great patience and careful instruction.

Finally, as the body of Christ we are called to build one another up in our walk, provoking one another toward a deeper faith in God. In doing so, we are to seek the good of our fellow believers and not search for ways to tear them down. If we see another believer who is struggling, we need to lift them up, as Paul reminds us:

Romans 15:1-4
¹We who are strong ought to bear with the failings of the weak and not to please ourselves. ²Each of us should please his neighbor for his good, to build him up. ³For even Christ did not please himself but, as it is written: "The insults of those who insult you have fallen on me." ⁴For

everything that was written in the past was written to teach us, so that through endurance and the encouragement of the Scriptures we might have hope.

Don't misunderstand this as a suggestion that those involved in the ECM are inherently the weaker brothers. That may be true in some cases, but it would be a false assumption to say that is the case for all. In fact, those who are strong enough to stand firm for Christ in the face of a postmodern culture may well be the stronger and more mature believers. What I am suggesting here is that we need to look toward building each other up in love regardless of where we are ministering. Everyone can learn more and grow closer to God. But no one will do so if they are not built up in the truth. Paul and Barnabas spent an entire year with the church at Antioch, teaching them and building them up in their faith. The work that they put in had such an impact that the people around these believers began to call them "Little Christs", or Christians.

The work of building up the faith of others also falls squarely within the great commission:

> **_Matthew 28:19-20:_**
> [19]Therefore go and <u>make disciples</u> of all nations, baptizing them in the name of the Father and of the Son and of the Holy Spirit, [20]and <u>teaching them to obey everything I have commanded you.</u> And surely I am with you always, to the very end of the age." (emphasis added)

Mutual edification is the completion of the work of evangelism. But there is also a negative side to edification. We are not only to build others up by teaching them what is right, we are also commanded to stop people from teaching what is wrong and leading others down the wrong paths. Once again, I believe that balance is essential in all of this. I would not wish to call people to become "heresy hunters" and to start our own version of the Inquisition. However, I believe we would be well served to consider the words of Thomas Oden:

> "Although I concede that there are other tasks more important than the exposure of heresy, I warn: If there is no immune system to resist heresy, there will soon be nothing but the teeming infestation of heresy"[2]

And so we also need to act as Paul charged both Timothy and Titus:

1 Timothy 1:3-7
[3]As I urged you when I went into Macedonia, stay there in Ephesus so that you may command certain men not to teach false doctrines any longer [4]nor to devote themselves to myths and endless genealogies. These promote controversies rather than God's work—which is by faith. [5]The goal of this command is love, which comes from a pure heart and a good conscience and a sincere faith. [6]Some have wandered away from these and turned to meaningless talk. [7]They want to be teachers of the law, but they do not know what they are talking about or what they so confidently affirm.

---

[2] Thomas C. Oden, "The Real Reformers are Traditionalists", *Christianity Today*, February 9, 1998, pg. 45

> **Titus 2:1**
> *You must teach what is in accord with sound doctrine.*

As I stated at the beginning of this book, I believe the true danger posed by the ECM is that it has the potential to create just another religious system full of good but empty works and devoid of a true faith and a real relationship with God. There will always be people who can rally others to join a cause, but to transform the soul takes an act of the living God. The role of the church is to stand between the two, and serve as God's representatives and ambassadors in this fallen world. The church itself can and should make constant adjustments in the way that it interacts with the world, but those changes should never take place at the expense of the truth, the gospel, or the scriptures. We need to be a light in the darkness of our world, and we must keep that light as bright and pure as possible.

As we consider our response to the Emerging Church Movement, we should not be afraid of new thoughts and ideas, but we must test them against the truth of the Scriptures before we consider adopting them into our own churches and our homes. We cannot stop the changes in the world, nor can we let the world slip by us while we remain mired in our old ways. Holding fast to the gospel and the scriptures does not require us to become outdated and insensitive – just the opposite. It requires us to work harder and think even more clearly in order to reach this ever-changing sin bound world, so that they too can realize the joy of truly knowing our God and Savior. Therefore, let us encourage one another toward that very end. May God be glorified by our proper response.

Index of Scriptures

Reference	Page	Reference	Page
Genesis 3:1-6	55	Philippians 1:9-11	103
Matthew 7:13	105	1 Timothy 1:3-7	120
Matthew 7:13-14	85	1 Timothy 3:13-16	115
Matthew 7:21-23	85	1 Timothy 6:3-5	114
Matthew 7:22-23	67		
Matthew 28:19-20	119	2 Timothy 2:15	115
		2 Timothy 3:14-15	115
Luke 11:9-10	41	2 Timothy 3:14-17	88
		2 Timothy 3:14-18	53
John 14:6	42, 85	2 Timothy 3:16-17	110
John 17:17	42	2 Timothy 4:2	118
John 18:37-38	31	2 Timothy 4:3-4	9, 75, 113
John 6:26	93		
John 6:26-27	96	Titus 2:1	121
Acts 11:19-26	110	Hebrews 11:1	47
Acts 17:11	7, 116	Hebrews 5:11 - 6:1a	53
Acts 28:1-6	62		
Acts 4:12	70, 105	James 2:14-18	57, 65
		James 2:19	83
Romans 1:16	108		
Romans 14:19	118	2 Peter 1:16-21	78
Romans 15:1-4	118	2 Peter 1:20-2:3	43
Romans 16:25-27	91	2 Peter 1:20-21	110
1 Corinthians 1:18	108		
1 Corinthians 13:1-3	87		
1 Corinthians 9:20-22	49		

About the author:

Ron Wright lives with his wife, Wendi, and their three children in Chesapeake, Virginia. Ron graduated from Cedarville College (now Cedarville University) in 1993, majoring in both Finance and Accounting with a minor in Biblical Studies. Ron and Wendi have continually been active in their local church. Ron has served as a part-time youth pastor, teacher, and deacon. In 2001 Ron and Wendi helped to start a new church plant in Portsmouth, Virginia, where Ron worked as an administrative leader and worship pastor.

Ron and Wendi currently attend Colonial Baptist Church in Virginia Beach, Virginia, where they are actively involved in various aspects of the ministry. Both are involved with the music ministry and Ron works with the student ministry leading worship in their weekly services. Wendi is active with the AWANA children's ministry and serves as a member of the leadership team for the various women's ministries as well. Ron is also a member of the advisory board for Central Baptist Theological Seminary of Virginia Beach.

Ron is the founder and president of Advantage Investing, Inc., a money management firm and registered investment advisor also located in Chesapeake, Virginia. He is a member of the CFA Institute and was awarded the CFA designation by the institute in the summer of 2006.

www.ingramcontent.com/pod-product-compliance
Lightning Source LLC
Chambersburg PA
CBHW020008050426
42450CB00005B/373